Baudrillard's bestiar

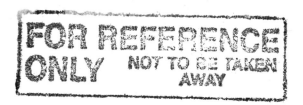
*The symbolic is neither a concept, nor an instance or a
category, nor a 'structure', but an act of exchange and a social
relation which points to an end to the real, which resolves the
real, and in the same stroke the opposition between the real
and the imaginary.*

Jean Baudrillard

This book provides an introduction to Baudrillard's cultural theory:
the conception of modernity and the complex process of simulation.
It examines his literary essays: his confrontation with Calvino,
Styron, Ballard, and Borges. It offers a coherent account of
Baudrillard's theory of cultural ambience, and the culture of
consumer society. It also provides an introduction to Baudrillard's
fiction-theory, and the analysis of transpolitical figures.

The book also includes an interesting and provocative comparison
of Baudrillard's powerful essay against the modernist Pompidou
Centre in Paris and Fredric Jameson's analysis of the Bonaventure
Hotel in Los Angeles. An interpretation of this encounter leads to
the presentation of a very different Baudrillard from that which
figures in contemporary debates on postmodernism.

Informative and consistently challenging, this book will be of
interest to students of Sociology and Cultural Studies.

Mike Gane is Senior Lecturer in Social Sciences at Loughborough
University.

Baudrillard's bestiary

Baudrillard and culture

Mike Gane

London and New York

First published 1991
by Routledge
11 New Fetter Lane, London EC4P 4EE

Simultaneously published in the USA and Canada
by Routledge
a division of Routledge, Chapman and Hall, Inc.
29 West 35th Street, New York, NY 10001

© 1991 Mike Gane

Typeset in English Times
by Pat and Anne Murphy, Highcliffe-on-Sea, Dorset
Transferred to digital printing 2003

British Library Cataloguing in Publication Data
Gane, Michael, *1943–*
    Baudrillard's bestiary: Baudrillard and culture.
    1. French Philosophy. Baudrillard, Jean
    I. Title
    194

Library of Congress Cataloging in Publication Data
Also available

ISBN 0–415–06306–X
        0–415–06307–8 (pbk)

I once met someone on a busy train in France, sitting opposite, reading a book by Baudrillard, the same book I was reading myself.
This book is dedicated to the memory of the shared enthusiasm of our discussion . . .

and to all lost friends.

Is it necessary to refer to Hölderlin's verses on salvation rising on the horizon of maximum peril?

Tafuri

fateful moments exist only in bad novels, and past and future it knows only in curious variations

Benjamin

Contents

Acknowledgements

I would like to thank all the many people with whom I have discussed and argued issues raised in this book, but especially Chris Rojek of Routledge who initially persuaded me of the importance of the project and who offered encouragement throughout; also friends and colleagues at Loughborough University, in the Departments of both Social Sciences and European Studies, who have provided expert opinion and critical commentary. I have also given a paper on Baudrillard to seminars at Essex University and Edinburgh University, and to the Discourse and Rhetoric Group at Loughborough University and would like to thank these seminars for their debates. I have also discussed these issues with colleagues on the editorial board of the journal *Economy and Society*, especially Beverley Brown and Ali Rattansi. I would like to thank Monique Arnaud not only for help with French translations, but also with essential critical discussion on all aspects of this project. Finally, I would like to thank Jean Baudrillard for generously responding to my queries. As is customary and essential, it is necessary to stress that responsibility for any error of fact or interpretation is entirely mine.

Introduction
The double infidelity

*He must . . . take upon himself the weight of the double
infidelity*

Blanchot

Baudrillard's work represents an attempt to establish a general
theory of two fundamental social forms. In one sense it is an
evident attempt to rewrite Durkheim's two basic social formations
(segmental, organized). But Baudrillard's relation to Durkheim is
certainly not direct, and, if Baudrillard is fundamentally Durkheimian, this is apparent only in displacement, repositioning, total
revision. In a sense, however, to regard Baudrillard from this point
of view is extremely enlightening. It could be said that what
Baudrillard wants to do is to convert the main focus of analysis
away from types of social solidarity to two basically opposed forms
of culture. There are immediate difficulties in posing the problem
in these terms however, and even Baudrillard struggles to maintain
a consistent vocabulary. For, at his most consistent, primitive
societies do not have cultures. Their societies are lived in the
symbolic, and in symbolic exchange. Theirs is a society of 'us' and
outsiders (others, gods, animals). Ours is a universal society of the
human: it is the latter universe which strictly speaking is 'culture',
and its other is the inhuman (1976: 193). Baudrillard develops this
distinction through increasingly radical forms.

   It is not easy to describe or identify precisely Baudrillard's point
of departure or fundamental position in this project. It is facile to
suggest that he simply supports the position of the primitive against
culture. It is only slightly more sophisticated to argue that he is best
interpreted as a Nietzschean surveying the disenchanted world with

aristocratic disdain. Although it is probably still grossly inadequate as a description, it seems that his position is very close to that of a modern Hölderlin of whom Blanchot has written:

> Today the poet no longer has to stand between gods and men as their intermediary. Rather he has to stand between the double infidelity; he must keep to the intersection of this double – this divine and human – reversal. This double and reciprocal movement opens a hiatus, a void which must henceforth constitute the essential relation of the two worlds. The poet, then, must resist the pull of the gods who disappear and draw him toward them in their disappearance. He must resist pure and simple subsistence on the earth which poets do not found. He must accomplish the double reversal, take upon himself the weight of the double infidelity and thus keep the two spheres distinct, by living the separation purely, by being the pure life of the separation. For this empty and pure space which distinguishes between the spheres is the sacred, the intimacy of the breach which is the sacred.
>
> (Blanchot 1982: 274)

This idea captures better than any other the tension of Baudrillard's poetic practice (Hölderlin is cited, 1976: 239).[1] What Baudrillard attempts, in an unsentimental manner, is to live in a world in which God has left either because He has died or because He has turned his back on it. Baudrillard keeps symbolic forms alive, and his infidelity is practised towards the present. Thus the pathos in Baudrillard is not as intense as in Hölderlin, since, at least at the crucial stage of Baudrillard's development, he wanted to remain faithful to the idea of the symbolic order.

But what exactly is the symbolic order? Here Baudrillard's ideas have developed. In 1976, he suggested:

> the symbolic is neither a concept, nor an instance or a category, nor a 'structure', but an act of exchange and a social relation which puts an end to the real, which resolves the real, and in the same stroke the opposition between the real and the imaginary.
>
> (1976: 204)

(Later even the idea of social relation itself is identified as inappropriate and replaced with the notion of symbolic tie: an inexorable process of radicalization of the divergence between orders of symbolic ties and cultures of social relations.) In his earlier discussion the major concept which carried the weight of the critique of the sign was that of ambivalence. In one statement Baudrillard gave it the power to check the sign itself:

> Only ambivalence (as rupture of value, of another side or beyond of sign value, and as the emergence of the symbolic) sustains a challenge to the legibility, the false transparency of the sign.
>
> (1972, 1981b: 150)

This has to be understood, as Baudrillard noted, in the sense that the symbolic process, thus conceived, is a radical alternative to the 'concept of the sign and to signification' (1972: 149). The sign is defined as the crystallization of the signifier and signified, and although this can be realized on the field of polyvalence (1972: 150) it cannot tolerate ambivalence. The basic dilemma is well grasped by Baudrillard: how is it possible to talk of the symbolic except through a modality which renders it null (1972, 1981b: 161)?

The Saussurean notion of the referent (the real object) is also given sharp treatment:

> this perceptual content . . . is shifted to the level of the sign by the signified, the content of thought. Between the two, one is supposed to glide in a kind of frictionless space from the perceptual to the conceptual, in accordance with the old recipes of philosophical idealism and the abstract associationism that was already stale in the 19th century.
>
> (1972, 1981b: 153)

In fact, perhaps the whole of Baudrillard's project can be located around this attack on the illusion of the referent.

By 1976 a number of significant developments in Baudrillard's position had occurred, which make it much less difficult to understand the main lines of theoretical critique. After all it is extremely difficult to grasp just what the nature of ambivalence as a characteristic of society can possibly mean. By 1976 the full importance of Saussure's analyses of anagrams had become widespread in the writing of Starobinski and the Tel Quel group, especially Julia Kristeva. This enabled Baudrillard to broaden his theory and to move away from a dependence on the notion of ambivalence.

Baudrillard's argument for an anti-materialist theory of language begins with a critique of materialism as a simple inversion of idealism, which renders idealism a service. So it would be wrong to conclude that Baudrillard wants to present an idealist theory; his critique could well render materialism a service. In the theory of the sign as adopted in psychoanalysis there is, he argues, always in fact a yielding of the sign to a positive analogy of the thing signified: for example, the unconscious appears as language disorder. And

> it is the blind, transversal surreality of the libido which comes to burst the reality principle and transparency principle of language. This is how, under the best circumstances, poetry is interpreted as transgression.
>
> (1981c: 79–80)

What occurs is often a form of metaphor or condensation. In the theatre of cruelty (Artaud) there is a liberation of a force but only in the form of metaphor: the repressed is released as content. Even Lyotard's notion of the rhythmic harmonization of the thing and the word through the intervention of the body is only another version of this materialism (1981c: 80–1).

The only way out of this dilemma, says Baudrillard, is to conceptualize the poetic as placing the relative positions of words and things into question by volatizing them: it should aim at the destruction of signification, the extermination (in a sense to be defined) of language, as discourse and as materiality. Thus Baudrillard introduces some important new terms: extermination, annihilation, poetic resolution.[2] The symbolic process (or, as he calls it, the symbolic operation) does not appeal to a material base, or a referent, or a hidden unconscious. It operates like anti-matter, without being ideal. This is similar to Saussure's notion of poetic cancellation: the poetic rhythm of vowel and counter-vowel conceived as a cancellation not as an accumulation. In the end there is no remainder. Baudrillard cites Kristeva's analysis of Greek poetry which concludes that these poems do not express the world, they are the world (1976: 339), and that

> In that other place, where the logical laws of language are shaken off, the subject is dissolved and in the place of the sign, it is the collision of signifiers annihilating each other that takes over. It is an operation of generalised negativity which has nothing to do with the negativity that constitutes judgement (Aufhebung) or with the negativity internal to judgement (0–1 logic) – it is a negativity that annihilates (Buddhism – sunyavada). A zero-logical subject, a non-subject that comes to assume this thought that annihilates itself.
>
> (Kristeva, cited in Baudrillard 1981c: 81)

But Baudrillard is not only a poet, or only a theorist of the sign. His first major work was a study of the new culture of consumer capitalism, in which he identified a new ambience in the world of objects. This work, *The Object System* (1968), was the beginning of a number of sociological investigations into the cultures of modern western capitalist societies. It is the rigour, even the obsession, with which he persisted in these reflections which mark his work. The driving theme of this project was the remarkable inversion of all previous expectations, especially for Marxists, in the emergence of affluent consumer societies. The radical analysis of these societies had to begin, he insisted, with the fact that it was through consumer affluence that social integration in a class-divided society was now being achieved. It was not predominantly through the physical power of the state or of work, but rather through the seductive power of an ambient culture that the society's discipline was maintained. The main enemy, for the left, had changed, and it was essential, Baudrillard maintained, to reconstruct social theory to take account of it. This led to a full-scale theoretical investigation in a work called *The Consumer Society* (1970), combining semiological with sociological and psychoanalytic styles of analysis. But, after a period of critical self-reflection following the defeat of May '68, his analysis broke out of its Marxist confinement and greatly radicalized both the conception of non-utilitarian cultures based on the organizing principle of symbolic exchange and the critique of capitalist cultures also based on it. This deepening was thus two-fold: it elaborated new ways of thinking about symbolic exchange in the anagram, in the poetic, in the significance of rituals of birth and death; and it reconstructed its critique of modern societies as it located new forms of resistance within the affluence, the fatal strategies of the silent majorities. The unity of Baudrillard's project is thus remarkable – from an analysis of ambience, of a change in the dominant form of power into the object, his work moves to an analysis of changing forms of resistance to it in the consuming masses: a mode of resistance that takes the very form of the subject as an object (passive, silent, hyperconformist). In a final twist of the spiral of his work, he broadens out the analysis of these forms of resistance into the world of objects in general: things themselves have silent strategies, and appear to offer to human action a vision of inhuman subversion.[3]

Chapter 2

From literary criticism to fiction-theory

One can never be sure of saving one's soul by writing

Calvino

Baudrillard's intellectual formation was decisively marked by literature, and it is no accident nor is it incidental that Baudrillard's first essays were literary in the traditional sense, and his first period was dominated by work of translation from German into French. However, the critical phase passed, and in the 1970s Baudrillard began to use literature more as a theoretical resource (and aesthetic criticism disappeared). In this chapter this transition is examined through close scrutiny of Baudrillard's changing techniques of reading fiction: first of a set of novels around 1962, second of J.G. Ballard's *Crash*, and last of Borges' story 'The Lottery in Babylon'.

ITALO CALVINO

Among Baudrillard's first publications was a set of critical reviews for *Les Temps Modernes* of recently published fiction by Calvino, Uwe Johnson, and William Styron. These reviews are interesting and relevant here, for they allow us a glimpse of Baudrillard's style and analytical orientations before he became an academic sociologist. These reviews, although relatively brief, reveal a writer with considerable grasp of literary and psychoanalytic theory, and an emerging maturity of social criticism dominated by a refusal both of simplistic solutions to the socialist project and of cynical rejections of the possibility of progressive engagement however charming or seductive their forms might be.

Among these pieces is a lucid and coherent review of three stories by Italo Calvino (recently taken by Salman Rushdie – Herbert Read Lecture – as paradigmatic of the human condition). The stories centre, in order, on a viscount (a story recalled by Baudrillard thirty years later, 1989e: 66), a baron, and a knight, and are generally set in a period of the decline of chivalry. The story of the viscount is, according to Baudrillard, a kind of *fantasie bouffe*, a cruel baroque fantasy: in the war against the Turks a viscount is cut in two by a canonball. One part, on returning home, terrorizes the countryside splitting all the things and beings he finds in two. The other part is virtuous and repairs all the damage caused by the other. In the end, 'Hoffmanesque' says Baudrillard, the two halves fight a duel and are miraculously rejoined.

The Baron in the Trees is set in a larger scenario (the Napoleonic wars in Italy). A young nobleman is forced to eat snails against his will by his parents and decides to rebel and to take to living in the trees. A fine 'Robinsonade', says Baudrillard of this 'arboreal solitude', but a Robinsonade lived passionately. It is rich in the symbolism of exile. The final story is that of *The Non-existent Knight*, told by a nun of the adventures of Agiluf, the empty suit of armour, who is none the less a personality, this time not passionate but a 'passive allegory of absence', responding to a challenge to protect the honour of woman he has previously saved from rape. If the pleasure is more in the pure enjoyment of reading than in reflection on its meaning, said Baudrillard, here is a literature of pure charm: instead of Don Quixote here is pure abstraction. But the empty armour is obsessed with detail and perfection, as if practising a methodical 'pharisaical' ritual of a dying caste. He is the sign of a dying and lifeless world, but obsessed with verification of givens: he disinters bodies, verifies sauces, but is bored and morose. He strikes out at the derisory bats which are none the less, unlike him, vividly alive; he longs for a body of his own.

The stories are clear and seductive, but criticisms can be made on a number of levels. Agiluf poses some problems since there appears a fine irony in a knight in all his fine armour who cannot possess women as he has no body. Yet Calvino paradoxically makes him the object of a subtle erotization, and women come to idolize their hero. He thus appears exalted and romanticized. Yet the hero is an empty impotence, even coming to imply the political disenchantment of an abstracted void. What could be the significance of this for Calvino? asks Baudrillard. Another basic problem arises with the baron, since, as soon as real historical elements enter into the scene, for example, when the baron condescends to aid the revolutionary armies from the trees, the writing becomes, says Baudrillard, less convincing, and it appears that Calvino cannot engage with revolutionary historical truth (a style suitable to describing the Franks and the Saracens is no longer adequate to deal with peasant insurrection). The stories have irony but also a dissonance, a stylistic fault, arising from false and forced solutions. But there are successful characters and these tend to be the romantic ones. Take Bradamante in the knight's story: her affection moves from the void to a real knight (Raimbaut). And perhaps this is Calvino's own view, the transcendence of absence towards well-being. A charming conception, says Baudrillard.

The question of the void is a genuinely modern problem, Baudrillard continues, but if Calvino attacks it with Italian brio, the style itself is passive, lacks attack and aggression. The story even appears as a pleasant chase; the reader senses that the pleasures of writing dominate those of construction. The stories thus appear as the result of highly cultivated writing, even a kind of surrealism, but this has a weakness: the characters, perhaps like the author, are simply engaged in a daily round of search for happiness, and each must find it on his own. For Calvino, however, perhaps even the writer's search for images is not an unalloyed pleasure, something of the charm of writing has disappeared. He perhaps feels nostalgia for it just as the knight feels nostalgia for his own body. As Bradamante says, 'one can never be sure of saving one's soul by writing. One may go on writing with a soul already lost' (Calvino 1962: 72). Baudrillard warns that we should perhaps be careful, therefore, not to be taken in by the charms of Calvino's writing.

UWE JOHNSON

Uwe Johnson's *Speculations about Jakob* (1959, English translation 1963) was also the subject of a critical review. The book weaves speculations around the death of an East German railway dispatcher, an event which begins the book. In part the book is narrative, but its major sections are statements by the principal characters, Jakob's family, friends and Rohlfs, a bureaucratic figure involved in security surveillance. Baudrillard notes that the family relations themselves are already more than usually complex (involving adoption) and the mother is effectively always absent.

Jakob's sister (by adoption) works in the west as a translator (for NATO) which gives rise to possibilities, real or imaginary, of espionage. The time of the action is the period leading up to and involving the Hungarian uprising; this brings Jakob's sister (Gesine) to the east. Their relationship is intensified but becomes more problematic with the arrival of Jonas (a lecturer at the university in East Berlin, who leaves his job), who is in love with her (they had met in the west). The political and moral problem is that of the border: on which side in principle and in fact should one live? Gesine returns to the west and is visited by Jakob. He refuses to stay, finding the west unacceptable. He is found dead, hit by a train in the fog, at his place of work.

Baudrillard views the book as a political autopsy, dissecting the meaning of the death of Jakob on many levels (though there are many ambiguous elements, such as the real activity of Gesine). But the central mystery is not the ominous bureaucratic activity of Rohlfs, but the character of Jakob himself, incomprehensible to the western mind. The book becomes a series of accounts of the life of Jakob; here Johnson's methods eschew purely ideological, psychological, or historical interpretations. For Baudrillard, Johnson's own method seems uncannily like those of Jonas in the book; he is a meticulous philologist who says of his work

> philology deciphers, discloses in early scrolls the long-since forgotten words by way of better known quotations in other preserved writings; it compares dictionary grammars maps excavations fauna and flaura of the probable landscape. It retraces the order that ruled declensions and syntax; each dialect has its special dictionary with grammatical appendix. One searches among the various versions of a text for the seemingly most authentic (least corrupted).
>
> (Johnson 1963: 80, trans. mod.)

The meaning of the intertextuality of Johnson's book is sustained by the life of Jakob; it is developed in a detached and empirical style reminiscent of the contemporary positivist human sciences. It implies the refusal to conjecture beyond the facts, and obsessively accumulates all possible facts. Ironically, says Baudrillard, it is itself a kind of literary dispatching on multiple rails. Perhaps, he says, to this complex 'polygraphy' of the book, further details could be added in the style of a philologist. But would this method ever produce the desired result? For the problem is that Johnson's method produces accounts only in the mode by which human relations are reduced to objects: his characters are lifeless.

But Johnson maintains a high, romanesque division between good and evil. He appears to produce a melancholy identification with, and literary sublimation in, his own characters. Jakob is tracked up to the point of his irreconcilability with the social order. At least Johnson dares to provide a black poetry, Baudrillard remarks, and not some neat ideological or psychological resolution. The ground of the book is the metaphysical rupture of Germany into two parts (parallel to Faulkner's black and white), and this inflects each gesture, each object. It is a distance and a gravity which raises in Johnson, Baudrillard suggests, a 'new problematic of description' – for even a tree is 'a tree-beyond-the-border', and everything is politicized, not as an element of suspense, but as an integral to the gaze of the book.[1] As Baudrillard notes, it is not, for Johnson, the eyes in themselves as essential organs which give expression, it is their environment (skin, muscles, eyebrows, etc.). So he seeks to find, in the life of this East German worker, the secret of a new fundamental 'fracture' in modern society – in this case not directly black/white, or good/bad, but, here, east/west – of which Jakob's death is the expression.

Baudrillard's discussion of Johnson's novel suggests that here the problem is badly posed and insufficiently worked through. The character of Jonas, he observes, is particularly weakly drawn and unconvincing.

Baudrillard subjects the system of familial relations depicted in the novel to close scrutiny from a psychoanalytic point of view. As in the case of other novels by Uwe Johnson, he suggests, the mother is absent or lost, even described at one point by Jakob as 'like death'. The effect of this absence is to produce an intensification of certain other relations, especially the brother–sister relation, and a reappearance of antagonistic relations to 'symbolic fathers' (behind Rohlfs, the state). The socialist state appears as a constraining and suspicious paternal reality, but without palpable reality beyond Jakob. The state appears as procreator, protector, yet is hostile and frustrated: socialism, thus approached, appears as a paternalist form of affective bonding, never, says Baudrillard, as a form of class solidarity. In the relation between Jakob and Rohlfs what is portrayed is a version of the politicization of a particular system of oedipal relations, an intense interweaving of familial and political sentiments. Thus the death of Jakob is the sign of a radical discrepancy in the divided family and society, and so implicates the west profoundly.

But the 'sign' of the dislocation between this man and his means of action, between this man and citizen, is Gesine. She is the active agent in bringing things together and separating them. Bonded to her family in the east she is an accomplice to the west. But she is never dramatized, nor are bonds of love erotized. Gesine possesses a liberty central to the thesis of the book. At the end, the curtain falls and she is alone. Thus Baudrillard's critique identifies a fatal overdetermination of the problem of socialism by Johnson's illegitimate insertion into the problematic of a particular, unresolved, oedipal antagonism.

But it is clear, for Baudrillard, that what is at stake in the novel is the definition of socialism in the East German state. At heart, the issue is an interrogation of 'socialist man', but having as its starting point an objective system of descriptions in which Jakob appears as mediator of the terms of contradiction. Johnson, here, is a specific type of literary craftsman, attempting to open up problems through a critical use of words. If it is useful to apply the concept of objectivity in this sense to objects, it does not appear to work, Baudrillard stresses, in the case of human relations (which remain in this piece utterly impenetrable. All the human beings in this novel appear complete strangers to each other, and any historical dimension the novel might aspire to vanishes.) Essentially, praxis cannot be described because it does not pertain to the domain of exactitude. Johnson always begins to work, says Baudrillard in admiration, with a critical attitude to definitions, to disrupt previous definitions. As with Jonas, 'organisation of things begins with lexical disorganisation'. From the critique of the ideological givens of things, he moves to the critique of ideological conversations. There is, nevertheless, says Baudrillard, a freshness in these descriptions; they are exempt from all artificial and imposed values.

What is suggested, in this novel, is not a new socialist realism nor a sentimental return to the collectivity. Here there is a new praxis of transformation, an open materialism linked to the orientation of things themselves without any presumption of ultimate meaning. Political objectives as such are not in view; the technique appears absolutely class-indifferent. Indeed, in the place of any meaningful ideology Johnson inserts, without romanticism, a 'functionality without regret'; liberty remains conjectural. But, even so, the science has a political sense, since it is implied here that rational technique, responsibility, moral integrity are sufficient to establish socialism. The celebration of practice may compensate for political alienation. In Johnson, there is an optimistic tone in the description of things, and this is quite in contrast to the account of human relations. Baudrillard comments, acidly, it is as though in this society people are weary of personal gods, and they have in consequence been brought to earth. Johnson, weary of (state) dogmatism and determinism, but with respect for rationality, has 'recorded his socialism in objects and their use'. His socialism is therefore a species of craft or artisanal Marxism, a concern for detail, a 'distrust for higher instances'. Remote from revolutionary Marxism this is a practice concerned with technical action on the world, and its exact signification and recording. Johnson believes that this method is appropriate because all human praxes are formally identical in all domains. And this is what literature must become, a concrete means of perpetual criticism and demonstration, an idea, Baudrillard notes, not far from that of Goethe or Brecht.

Thus Baudrillard's reading is nuanced and balanced. It is clear that the analyses, aesthetic, psychoanalytic, and political, are directly articulated. What is striking is the latent humanist elements of Baudrillard's assessment, and certainly of his clear attempt to avoid any schematic pigeonholing of Johnson's position. Although the review begins with criticism of Johnson's objectivism, by the end it is clear that Baudrillard thinks this has possibly saved Johnson from rehashing ideological commonplaces.

WILLIAM STYRON

The final review in this group concerned William Styron's *Set This House on Fire*, which Baudrillard reads as a corrosive displacement of the social struggle of the American south into a post-war Italian context. Its central characters are two Americans, Mason (from north of the Mason–Dixon line) and Cass (from Carolina). The former is wealthy and lives in a state of Dionysian debauchery; the latter, a down-at-heel artist and alcoholic who despises American crassness, has to provide Mason with pornographic paintings. Cass aids an Italian peasant family and dreams of a romance with the peasant's daughter Francesca. Mason rapes her, and her Italian lover kills her. The book, in Baudrillard's review, is read as an account, written in the 'most visionary, baroque and puritan, style' (unlike that of Faulkner, or any possible aristocratic melancholy), of the lived culpability of Cass who in a moment of outrage kills Mason. Baudrillard reads it as a concrete psychological study leading to a sustained critique of American 'deculturation' and of the unresolved tensions in current American society.

Even in the arrival of American cars in the novel, the sports car of Di Lieto and Mason's Cadillac, Baudrillard sees a kind of 'baptism of evil'. Cass reviles American crassness as it is manifested in material wealth and cultural crudity, and his murder of Mason produces an intensely ambivalent sense of guilt. But where others have seen a direct parallel between Cass and Raskolnikov, Baudrillard makes the parallel between Mason and Stavrogin (*The Possessed*). And just as epilepsy for Dostoevsky is a fatal sign, drunkenness here is not just a sign of moral destruction, it even becomes the lived form of alienation in a society enervated by leisure but remaining puritanical and 'pharisaical' to the highest level (previously subject of social ceremonial, here drunkenness has become the inverse sign of collective energies lost in a society too quickly industrialized). Mason himself is not, says Baudrillard, simply the incarnation of evil – too crude a concept. He is, rather, 'like a white surface' which reflects culpability. The murder is felt as a kind of deliverance, yet the book is an exploration of the problem of evil and the extent to which Cass was right to do what he did. Baudrillard's reading of the book concludes that for Styron the question is not resolvable if posed absolutely (as it is in the first half of the book). It becomes possible to think it through only on the basis of an examination of the lived ambiguity of the Cass–Mason relation and the relation to the peasant family (Styron sees, says Baudrillard, that, like the oedipal relation, violence always has three characters). But Cass is not a simple figure, for his reluctance to seduce Francesca is in part due to the fact that he himself is obsessed with the fear of raping her; his relation to Mason is one of ambivalent half-hate, half-admiration. His guilt is thus compounded. Styron's thesis then, according to Baudrillard, is that the murder is not a fatal outcome, but meaningful as shared conduct, an exchange of guilt, accessible to Styron as a lived responsibility. As for the writing itself, Baudrillard judges it to lack the quality of 'sudden denouement' that is the mark of style.

It is certainly an irony that Baudrillard has recently been identified as having all the marks of an aristocratic Nietzschean (Kellner 1989: 230), for this is precisely how the character Mason describes and identifies himself.

So now with art in a decadent stasis society must join in the
Dionysian upswing toward some spiritual plateau that will allow
a totally free operation of all our senses . . . what you don't seem
to realise Cassius, is how basically moral and even religious the
orgiastic principle is . . . floating bourgeois convention, that is, it
is a form of living dangerously – again Nietzsche . . . age-old
ritual . . . phallic thrust . . . ( ) . . . it's what the hipster and the
Negro know instinctively.

(Styron 1970: 424)

In his review Baudrillard rejects this view and its subsequent effects
as pathological.

It is clear then that these early reviews by Baudrillard are of
considerable interest in shedding light on the style and substance of
his thoughts in the early 1960s. There is a noticeable interest in
written style, balance, plot, compositional structure, suggesting a
background in literary studies, possibly of a fairly philosophical if
conventional kind. He is keen to reveal comparisons between
writers and between styles. Very obviously he works within a strict
set of oppositions: particularly that between baroque and roman-
esque/fantastic fiction. But these are always related to historical
and social context, the position of the social group in the historical
process. This implies a theory of social classes, particularly rising
or declining classes, as expressive of mood, philosophy, style of
life. There are here certainly the elements of Baudrillard's
sociology of literature, but accompanied by a psychoanalytic
approach to sexual and familial relations. His own position
certainly seems to be on the revolutionary left, but there is an interesting opposition to protestant and puritan cultural strains,
although this does not imply a catholic background. These come
together in the review of Styron in a remarkable attack on
American 'deculturation' and on the reduction of the Third World
to the state of 'negritude'. In this essay Baudrillard seems to
privilege existential responsibility over the impersonal action of
fate.

Is it possible to reconstruct Baudrillard's intellectual framework
in these years from these brief essays? In some respects it is
possible, for the essays are none the less rich in detail and observation, and in judgement. It is certainly possible to identify characteristic themes and orientations. In his engagement with literature
Baudrillard was interested in historical and moral questions, and

linked them, ultimately, to a Marxist and psychoanalytic problematic, one dominated by a conception of class relations and the
appropriateness of style to the literary representations of ascending,
ascendant and declining classes. These notions are not crudely
applied, and are articulated in a complex relation with interpersonal
analysis. Baudrillard's literary criticism does not look for moral
simplicities however: he excels in the critical elucidation of complex
social and moral situations, modernity made complex through the
interweaving of cultural and political division, and the accumulation of differential temporalities.[2]

J.G. BALLARD

These early reviews stand, however, in great contrast with the kind
of analysis adopted in the mid-1970s when Baudrillard came to
consider the novel *Crash* by J.G. Ballard (Baudrillard's essay first
appeared in 1976.) Here, superficially, some of Baudrillard's
previous critical vocabulary remains, for he describes Ballard's
writing as 'baroque and apocalyptic'. However, he is not now so
much concerned with the construction of the novel and its forms of
writing, as with the kind of world which is portrayed. Certainly by
this time Baudrillard himself had radically distanced himself both
from traditional revolutionary socialist positions and from the
theoretical traditions of Marxism and psychoanalysis. After Borges,
whose work is on a different level, Ballard, says Baudrillard, is the
first great novelist of the universe of simulation, of hyperreality.
Baudrillard reads the novel quite explicitly against the interpretation
of Ballard himself (who sees it in part as a moral story and a
warning).[3]

Traditionally, from Marx to McLuhan, Baudrillard argues, technology is viewed as an extension of the human body: it makes the
body more complex and increases its capacities. In *Crash*, this vision
is strikingly inverted and the picture which emerges is altogether
different from the heroic and Promethean world of progress in
depth. What is evident in this new world is not a functional
extension but a specific kind of deconstruction of the body, deconstruction unto death. This is not a simple story of social alienation
or even of the lost subject (as in psychoanalysis). It is a vision of the
body delivered in its symbolic wounds. In this novel the body is
literally fused with technology in all its clinical or surgical violence

(realized under the sign of a sexuality without limits). He cites Ballard:

> Her mutilations and death became a coronation of her image at the hands of a colliding technology, a celebration of the individual limits and facial planes, gestures and skin tones. Each of the spectators at the accident site would carry away an image of the violent transformation of this woman, of the complex wounds that fused together her own sexuality and the hard technology of the automobile. Each of them would join in his own imagination, the tender membranes of his own mucous surfaces, his groves of erectile tissue, to the wounds of this minor actress through the medium of his own motorcar, touching them in a medley of stylised postures. Each would place his lips on those bleeding apertures . . . press his eyelids against the exposed tendon of her forefinger, the dorsal surface of his erect penis against the lateral walls of her vagina. The automobile crash had made possible the final and longed-for union of the actress and the members of her public.
>
> (Ballard 1985: 145; Baudrillard 1981a: 166)

It is this fusion of the automobile and the body which catches Baudrillard's attention, as the complex pattern is built into a semiurgy where wounds become new sexual openings. Indeed, the body is a basis for a new series of anagrammatic mutilations. This marks, says Baudrillard, the end of erotic zones as such, as the body becomes the site of a new regime of abstract sign exchanges: body and automobile technology diffract each other. Not a story of the emotions or of psychology, nor of sado-masochism, nor even of a loss of meaning in sexuality, this is a novel where the savage reversibility of the body and technology brings a new 'non-sense', a new unlimited sexuality: the violent incisions are everywhere like graffiti in New York.

But the crucial move, says Baudrillard, is making the accident, hitherto perhaps marginal, and even in its irreversible forms somewhat banal, now the heart of the new system; no longer an exception, the accident becomes the rule. It now gives life. In this novel the automobile is the site of the action, where everything happens: tunnels, motorways, bridges, underpasses, overpasses. In this universe dysfunction seems to be a thing of the past, and with it perversion. The order of life portrayed is one which starts from death, and everything is reorganized from this principle. The accident is no longer a symptom, or a residue of transgression. It initiates, specifically, a 'non-perverse jouissance'.[4] The writing here he says, is quite different from that of Kafka (cf. *In the Penal Settlement*), for here death and sex are without metaphor, there is no trace of repression or puritanism. The technology of *Crash* is seductive, scintillating. The exchange of signs is so complete that the body and technology become inextricable:

> As Vaughan turned the car into a filling station courtyard, the scarlet light from the neon sign over the portico flared across these grainy photographs of appalling injuries: the breasts of teenage girls deformed by instrument binnacles, the partial mamoplasties . . . nipples sectioned by manufacturers' dashboard medallions; injuries to male and female genitalia caused by steering wheel shrouds, windshields during ejection. . . . A succession of photographs of mutilated penises, sectioned vulvas and crushed testicles passed through the flaring light. . . . In several of the photographs the source of the wound was indicated by a detail of that portion of the car which had caused the injury: beside a casualty ward photograph of a bifurcated penis was an inset of a handbrake unit; above a close-up of a massively bruised vulva was a steering wheel boss and its manufacturer's medallion. These unions of torn genitalia and sections of car body and instrument panel formed a series of disturbing modules, units of a new currency of pain and desire.
>
> (Ballard 1985: 104; Baudrillard 1981a: 169–70)

Thus it appears, says Baudrillard, that each mark is an artificial invagination, and only through this symbolic exchange of wounds does the body come into existence. On reflection, it is the accident of the natural simulacra that make up a sex. Here the wounds that become sexual do so anagrammatically. In primitive societies, sexuality is only one metaphor among many, and not the most significant. Here it has become an obsessional reference. In this particular story, all the sexual terminology is technical, there is no trace of popular argot or of informal intimacy. This language is technical and functional; there is an equalization of chrome and mucous membrane. Sperm has no more value than anything else. Sexual pleasure is confounded with a technological rhythm and its violence, and all revolves around the physicality of cars and their collisions. This system has no depth. The importance of the role of the photo and the cinema in the novel is to provide a mirror world.

The character of Vaughan himself classifies and orders photo-
graphs of accidents, not as a system of representation, nor as a
medium which transcends them: he is in no sense a voyeur. The
photograph is part of the hyperreal world itself: it gives it no extra
dimensions in time or space. 'The eye of the camera is the substitute
for time', says Baudrillard, in a universe without secrets.

The mannequin rider sat well back, the onrushing air lifting his
chin. His hands were shackled to the handlebars like a kami-
kaze's pilots. His thorax was plastered with metering devices. In
front of him, their expressions equally vacant, the family of four
mannequins sat in their vehicle. The faces were marked with
cryptic symbols.

A harsh whipping noise came towards us, the sound of the
metering coils skating along the grass beside the rail. There was a
violent metallic explosion as the motorcycle struck the front of
the saloon car. The two vehicles veered sideways towards the line
of startled spectators. I gained my balance, involuntarily holding
Vaughan's shoulder, as the motorcycle and its driver sailed over
the bonnet of the car and struck the windshield, then careered
across the roof in a black mass of fragments. The car plunged ten
feet back on its hawsers. It came to rest astride the rails. The
bonnet, windshield and roof had been crushed by the impact.
Inside the cabin the lopsided family lurched across each other, the
decapitated torso of the front-seat woman passenger embedded in
the fractured windscreen. . . . Shavings of fibreglass from its face
and shoulders speckled the grass around the test car like silver
snow, a death confetti. . . .

Helen Remington held my arm. She smiled at me, nodding
encouragingly as if urging a child across some mental hurdle.
'We can have a look at it again on the Ampex. They're showing it
in slow-motion.'
                        (Ballard 1985: 98; Baudrillard 1981a: 175–6)

In this book, therefore, the world is like a hypermarket, functional,
incessant, and a single live ambience. Yet, paradoxically, this functionality is cancelled out since it permits no dysfunctionality. In
exceeding its own limits, functionality becomes ungraspable,
ambivalent. Baudrillard comments, 'to parody Littre, in the pataphysical mode,[5] it is "a road that leads nowhere, but does so more
quickly than any other" '. But what really distinguishes this novel,
he says, is that it does not simply project the norms of our society

into the future, it does not live in the same world of purposes and lines of force. Here there is no more fiction or reality, the hyperreal annihilates them. Although sexual, this is a world without desire. It is full of violated and violent bodies, but they have become neutral. It is neither good or bad, it is simply high tech, without purpose: it has become fascinating, and should be viewed without value judgement. Baudrillard's last word is that the book achieves a miraculous form of writing in which the banality of violence is resolved in a vision without negativity.

Between Baudrillard's early critical essays, therefore, and this one, the world has indeed changed. Here Baudrillard finds not just a writer in a particular genre but a writer who vindicates his own vision, as long as the writer remains inside his novel. But certainly it is remarkable that Ballard's novel mirrors so completely Baudrillard's own thought down to its very terminology. The two writers have converged here quite spontaneously. It is certain that this is a result of the fact that both writers emerge from a psychoanalytic framework. Where Ballard has written what he imagines is a warning, Baudrillard accepts it as an account of the world as it is. But what is striking is the revolution in Baudrillard's vocabulary. What has been added is a new register of semiological and cultural theory, which has abolished the model in depth of Marx and Freud. It is also clear that in literary theory all models based on production and depth have also become obsolete (such as science fiction (1981a: 180)). Even the idea of criticism, and this is logical in the face of Baudrillard's new writing, has become a thing of the past. Thus Baudrillard is no longer interested in the portrayal of historical event, or of moral dilemma, or of character. The very specific impact of semiological theory seems to have coincided with an immense flattening out of the world.[6]

BORGES

Finally, this kind of appropriation of literature is continued in Baudrillard's reading (in *Seduction*, first published in 1979), of Borges's story 'The Lottery in Babylon' (Borges 1970: 55–61), which stresses the possibility that this story should be read not as fiction, but as 'a description that comes close to our former dreams, and that is to say to our future as well' (Baudrillard 1990a: 152). Thus, as with his response to Ballard, Baudrillard wants to flatten out any notion of literature as 'warning' or as philosophical interpretation of the world: the writing is a description. But what of Baudrillard's description of this story? Is it accurate? Although Ballard's 'novel' is long and Borges's story is only some six pages long, it is the short story which is more complex, and there is a sense in which Baudrillard perhaps does it some violence. Clearly and consistently with his whole approach – he does not leave any critical distance between himself and the text, for the story, or more accurately a particular reading of it, is urgently forced into the service of Baudrillard's own theses (a common way of reading Borges, see Gane (1989: ch. 5)). It is highly instructive, then, to compare the complexity of the story and the version Baudrillard presents to us, and to investigate what this might mean in relation to the fusion of theory and fiction in Baudrillard's new scheme,[7] and whether there is not a strong possibility that Borges has none the less out-trumped Baudrillard.

The story is told by a Babylonian about the 'institution' of the lottery in Babylon, but it is a condensed story since he is on the point of departure: his ship has already weighed anchor (Borges 1970: 58). (Thus in true Baudrillardian terms this story is a mode of disappearance.) The teller of the story admits he has already occupied all the major social statuses, experienced all the extremes of fate, since social life is determined not by a rigorous mechanism of continuous hierarchical reproduction, but by a lottery. The story he tells is a repetition of general historical knowledge about the lottery with some personal interjections and interpretations. The lottery developed, or so a tradition has it, out of the simple drawing of lots for money prizes, a popular game but one which was felt insufficient since it dealt only in money and hope. So, some forfeits were introduced in the form of financial penalties. This was organized by the Company. However the losers refused to pay and the Company was forced to convert financial penalties into custodial sentences so that the books could be balanced more sensibly. Obviously, the bravado of the non-payers was the 'source of the omnipotence of the Company and of its metaphysical and ecclesiastical power' (Borges 1970: 56). The Company converted the money forfeits into prison terms which introduced non-money elements into the game. Upper-class critics and the poor converged in their demand that money prizes should be converted as well and the game become free. This was confirmed in principle when a thief stole a draw ticket which turned out to be a physical forfeit: it was carried out not because of the theft or the status of the thief, but because of the principle of chance itself. But this inaugurated two things: the total power of the Company, since the scope and complexity of operations expanded dramatically to all areas of life, and, second, the extension of the lottery to 'all free men', as a free and secret drawing of lots every sixty nights. The chances were a mix of good (including social promotions) and bad (mutilations). But the Company became aware that the operation of pure chance limited its power, and a certain element of magic and suggestion was introduced. It resorted to undercover means of obtaining knowledge of the hopes of the people, and it refused to denounce rumours that there were certain avenues of information which led to the Company. There were then complaints that the Company had been influenced in the working of the lottery, to which it replied that errors may have been made but that error could not contradict chance, in fact it corroborated it.

The Babylonians, though conscious of the operations of fate, none the less speculated: perhaps it was logical that chance should be extended to all spheres, and this did lead to the decisive reform. There are now drawings of lots which give results which can be modified by further drawings. No decision at a draw is final or irreversible: each one branches out into larger actions, in principle to infinity. For example, a draw may indicate the decree of death, a further one that there are nine possible executioners, and each of the executioners makes a further draw which may reverse the decision or intensify it (adding torture to the sentence) and so on. There are also draws which act on the impersonal world, so that errors are wilfully introduced into events and things. At this point it becomes difficult to say whether an event is connected with the Company or not, or whether the omission in a book is a mistake or a deliberate calculation. There are also fake Companies which seek to introduce their own imitation errors into the flow of things.

Finally, there are a number of important opinions about the Company. It is suggested that it does not have a long past, since the sacred disorder in the world is a natural phenomenon, but others suggest that the Company has been an eternal form; yet others suggest that its sphere of action is limited and that only insignificant things are influenced by it. Others suggest that it has never existed, others still that it is useless to affirm or deny the existence of the lottery and the Company.

Such is Borges's story in outline. Baudrillard's version of the story skips over many points of the argument. It notes the introduction of the forfeit, which for Baudrillard 'radicalizes' everything (for Borges it is the conversion into the sentence which does this with its later transformations). Baudrillard immediately declares that the world enters a state of dizziness from this point, 'anything could happen by drawing lots' as the lottery became free, general and secret, and destinies were decided every sixty nights. This brought about the 'interpolation of chance in all the interstices of the social order' (1990a: 150) as even errors could be subsumed under the reign of chance. Henceforth no one could tell the difference between chance and manipulated events, and 'predestination encompassed everything'. Thus the Company, and the lottery, could even cease to exist, since the world and its simulation had become indistinguishable.

> At that point, it becomes a possibility that the Lottery or the Company have never existed at all, and it is only the assumption that they do which changes everything. These are cultures where reality enters into an immense simulacrum.
>
> (1990a: 151)

It is clear that Baudrillard has already, in effect, begun to interpret the story. He continues by comparing this situation, and these cultures, with our own in which the Company has ceased to exist. Our culture is oblivious to the possibility of total simulation, that is, where a spiral of simulation precedes reality, and so the sacred disorder is abandoned. Fate as a principle of the game already played is, for us, no longer a possible vision of the world. Yet this is the true content of our unconscious, not as individual field of repression, but as the repression of the symbolic order itself. Borges presents the principle of fate, of sacred disorder, as a radical principle of the determinant order of the social, and predestination brings total mobility, radical democracy, and even polyvalency. It reveals the principle of ritual, or the rule, or the pact as destructive of law, of contract, and of social relations. In principle all secret societies resist the social; these visions are cruel, but more profound as they are realized as destiny.

Finally, he argues, utilitarians and Marxists mock the games of chance which are found in Third World countries. But the idea that these games are inferior is wrong:

> Only the privileged, those elevated by the social contract or by their social status – itself only a simulacrum, and one without

even the value of a destiny – can judge such aleatory practices as
worthless when they are quite superior to their own.
(Baudrillard 1990a: 153)

Baudrillard's reading therefore is partial. Whereas Borges offers
multiple interpretations of the lottery, Baudrillard opts for one: the
penultimate of those offered by Borges (the Company has never
existed, only its myth is necessary). But Borges offers another, that
it is useless to affirm or deny the corporation (1970: 61).

This reveals that Baudrillard's position is not that of nihilism,
neither is it directly or naively that of aristocracy, for what is
omitted or suppressed in Baudrillard's version is the whole panoply
of the Company and its secret power. This is intimately linked to
the complicity of magic, influence, and the errors introduced by the
Company as fate. Thus Baudrillard misses the story's evocation of
the way the Company achieves omnipotence through complicity
with informers who reveal and therefore lead to the manipulation
of the hopes of the people as a resource (note that Borges subtly
implies that pure games of chance for money do not allow this
manipulation of chance, and that the sequence of events may have
become instigated by the Company itself). Baudrillard emphasizes
the fact that the lottery becomes secret, free, and general, but omits
to say that this is only the second consequence of the introduction
of the logic of the lottery: the first consequence is the ascent to total
power of the Company. He neglects to say that the social structure
of the society remains hierarchical: it is a slave society (there is a
strange contradiction between the radical democracy of the lottery
open to all 'free' men and the existence of slaves). Borges stresses
this right from the beginning of the story with the personal witness
of the narrator:

I have been proconsul; like all, a slave. . . . Look: the index
finger of my right hand is missing. . . . In the half light of dawn,
in a cellar, I have cut the jugular vein of sacred bulls before a
black stone. . . . In a bronze chamber, before the silent handker-
chief of the strangler, hope has been faithful to me, as has panic
in the river of pleasure.
(1970: 55)

In this slave society, according to Baudrillard, the institution of
the lottery introduces social reproduction by chance, a democratic
institution since all are equally bound by the draw. But the story

itself introduces a subtle play on the secret affinity of power and fate (as something that can be distinguished from chance), and the secret possibility of manipulation and its fusion with error. It certainly appears in the story that error is bad fortune. It is also claimed that 'historians have invented a method to correct chance' but this is not divulged without dissimulation: a whole secret practice (in which the story-teller himself is involved) of the introduction of errors and dissimulations into the world is positively cultivated with the effect that chance merges with deliberately created disorder under the manipulation of the Company. The silent functioning is comparable to that of God (and we might say the devil).

Thus Borges presents possibilities, even the possibility that the Company and the lottery have never existed, delightfully contradicting the express experience of the story-teller, whereas in Baudrillard there is only one flattened interpretation, forced in order to reach a pre-given theoretical analysis. Only on the basis of removing the features of a conspiratorial organization (and its line of communication to the hopes of the people through the sacred latrine, Qaphqa) can Baudrillard reach his conclusion, that 'predestination coincides here with a total mobility, and an arbitrary system with the most radical democracy' (1990a: 152). But Baudrillard's ultimate point, that our societies have lost the capacity to evoke this form of total simulation, requires merely the possibility, at some stage, of the myth of the Company – in order that the world is doubled.[8]

It is interesting to compare 'The Lottery in Babylon' with Kafka's (or Qaphqa's) short story 'The Problem of our Laws' (Kafka 1979: 128–30), which may even have influenced Borges. In this story, the laws are a secret of the small group of governing nobles: the story-teller notes that 'it is exceedingly distressing to be governed according to laws that one does not know'. In popular tradition the laws exist as a secret of the nobility and the nobility are above the law. Yet there is a counter-interpretation which differs from the popular one and which suggests that what the nobility does is the law, and the arbitrary acts of the nobility are all that are visible of the existence of the law. The issue cannot be decided, since there is insufficient knowledge. It may take centuries, but eventually, when there is sufficient knowledge, the laws will belong to the people.

Thus a paradox: the one visible and indubitable law is that it is imposed on us is the nobility, and could it really be our wish to deprive ourselves of this solitary law?

(Kafka 1979: 130)

Baudrillard's conception of the western world as it is today, perhaps, is of a world which has abolished the secret law, whether it is of the lottery, of the nobility, or of the secret bureaucracy. Baudrillard's vision is that of a progression, rather like that implied in Borges and Kafka: that history has moved through the stage where the secret institution was a vital principle, to a stage in which the arbitrary nature of events could still be understood to be influenced by its power. The final stage is the distancing of the events of the world from its reach altogether. But perhaps Baudrillard's own obsessions are visible in his reading of Borges: the hope that the fatal, vertiginous play of the game which gives rise to the sacred disorder, after being lost, makes its inevitable return. This is not a world, as is Borges's, of the labyrinth, of loss into an infinite play of mirrors, where its own form reduplicates in its branchings the possibility of infinite interpretation. Borges says of Kafka: his works are incomplete, and cannot be completed: their labour is infinite (in Kafka 1983: 6). Borges's stories are complete but can be infinitely subdivided or branched as in the lottery. Baudrillard's objective in his reading of the story by Borges is to establish the possibility of a contrast between the repetition to infinity of the flat, charmless universe of western culture and the closed but seductive, dizzy world of the infinite play of the sacred lottery: his writings begin an unending spiral of evocations of this single state where the game and fate fuse into destiny.

Chapter 3

Modern ambience of objects

repression in the advanced countries is not any more an aggression it is an ambience.

Baudrillard

THE MARXIST BACKGROUND

Baudrillard's problem towards the end of the 1960s was to establish a sociology of modern capitalist forms of consumption. His book *Le Système des Objets* ('The Object System') was published in 1968; he was later to call it phenomenological, and again, paradoxically, an exercise in critical structuralism.[1] This project certainly follows, but at a distance, Marx's own analysis of the commodity form and the subjection of social relations to the domination of this form. For Baudrillard, also, the analysis of new forms of wealth was to be a secondary question. What had to be analysed was not the emergence of new forms of proletarianization, nor the alienative effects of the labour process, nor of course new forms of immiseration or polarization. Baudrillard's critical attention was directly focused on new forms of consumption, the neglected later phases of the process of capitalist circulation. But consumption in Baudrillard's thought was not a passive end result of circuits of capital; rather it had become an active moment, possibly the crucial moment in the formation of new social relations, opening on to a new phase of capitalist development. Looked at in this light, Baudrillard's writings of this period constitute one of the very few attempts by major Marxist thinkers to engage in new social analysis.

Marx's own ideas, as developed in the later volumes of *Capital*, worth recalling briefly here, suggest the possibility of the internal evolution and 'negative' resolution of contradictions within capitalism. If the capitalist mode of production could be identified through such features as the existence of money, private ownership, merchant or financial capital, a labour market, and so on, it is clear that a fundamental feature is private individual capital. One of the most disputed aspects of Marxist theory is Marx's own very radical conception of the changes in economic practice in Britain in the mid-nineteenth century with the growth of joint stock companies. In Marx's view this development tended to put an end to the capitalist mode of production, not in a revolutionary dissolution of an oppressive system, but as a 'negative' resolution of an internal antagonism. 'It is the abolition of the capitalist mode of production within the capitalist mode of production itself, and hence a self-dissolving contradiction' (Marx 1966: 438). Marx saw this development as establishing new 'social' forms of property which he identified as transitional forms, a new phase, making possible co-operative movements and production on a large scale.

> The capitalist stock companies, as much as the co-operative factories, should be considered as transitional forms from the capitalist mode of production to the associated one, with the only distinction that the antagonism is resolved negatively in the one and positively in the other.
>
> (Marx 1966: 440)

Returning to this theme later in the book, he said,

> It does away with the private character of capital and this contains in itself, but only in itself, the abolition of capital . . . the credit system will serve as a powerful lever during the transition from the capitalist mode of production . . . but only as one element in connection with other great organic revolutions in the mode of production itself.
>
> (Marx 1966: 607)

Later in the history of Marxism this transformation was coded, by Lenin and Hilferding, as an internal change from the first to the second phase, the monopoly phase, of capitalism, dominated by finance capital.

In the 1960s a large number of new theories were being developed which attempted to deal with the emergence of capitalist affluence. A number of theories began to suggest the end of ideology, end of class, end of the proletariat, and so forth, or the end of the possibility of revolutions in the advanced economies. Barthes and Marcuse pioneered new theories of the 'negative' resolution of old contradictions, and of the new forms of welfare and social democracy in affluent post-war Europe. Notable was the attempt to analyse liberation and tolerance as 'repressive de-sublimination' and 'repressive tolerance'. These forms of liberation were controlled, managed, blocked, or reached a degree zero language, and led to new problems and new struggles, requiring new tactics. Just as the formation of joint stock companies had not resulted in the positive displacement of capitalist forms of exploitation and calculation, so these new developments left intact key oppressive structures. More than this there was a danger, for Marcuse, that the new forms of repression, lived as liberations, could compromise genuinely transcendent possibilities.

What Baudrillard attempted in his essays of this period could be expressed in terms similar to those adopted by Marcuse: 'repressive affluence and consumption', since he expressly approved of such terms as 'repressive needs'. Indeed, Baudrillard's writings in *Utopie* (1969a, 1969b) lead directly in this direction: 'repression in the advanced countries is not any more . . . an aggression, it is an ambience' (1969a: 3). In the new situation state power develops two aspects, both a maternal and a paternal (directly and physically) repression. This tends to the formation of pacified relations in everyday life and towards the erasure of the distinction between the 'ludic' and the 'policed'. It was a fundamental error of the students in May '68 to have seen the riot police as the principal agent of repression: this was to fall into the trap set by bourgeois society itself, of identifying repression with physical force or prohibition. In the turn to 'maternal' forms of control, oppression becomes the site of intense participation. And this is extremely difficult to grasp and to resist, especially in this case which seems more and more to work at the level of the image and the sign. Its effectiveness can even be seen in the transformation of the face of Paris, he observes, with the proliferation of boulevards devoted to spectacular consumption.

Baudrillard outlines a conception of new mechanisms of repression as involving separations and divisions in irreversible social orders: geographical, cultural, and professional. The totality of human desires is broken into fragments, into autonomous zones, private and public. This process tends to neutralize these zones as sites of potential contradiction. The private comes to appear as a domain for leisure and for personal realization. At their work, on the other hand, people escape by dreaming of freedom as lying on an (overcrowded) beach. The *category opposition of work and leisure replaces that of the work and the sacred*, a fundamental observation in Baudrillard's theory, allowing us to place his development directly in the French, Durkheimian, sociological tradition. Work, the social division of labour, is rarely experienced as a sphere of liberty. Even more important is a new division of human needs, in the face of pressure to abandon the set of previously established controls of the super-ego. The new enticements or incitements are not to a genuine and perhaps dangerous pleasure, but to the defusing, the measuring of pleasure to strictly proportioned repressive rituals of order.

These ideas seem consistent with Marcuse's view of contemporary alienation, but Marcuse does, at least when in an optimistic mood, call for a 'determinant negation' of the new order by a rational and collective pleasure system based firmly on basic human needs. For Baudrillard this idea is completely illusory. The idea of the 'revolution of needs', he says, is only in the end a modern version of 'idealist moral education' of the citizen, and will never 'offer a perspective of de-alienation . . . because needs as such are an immediate product of repression: parcellized, divided, disciplined'. There is a great risk here: the possibility of inscribing into the theory that which is already part of the repressive process.[2] Later in his career Baudrillard suggests that the analysis must strive to reach a point of departure beyond such processes. Here he insists that the true analysis of needs must always take off from the totality of the social divisions: the division of labour is fundamental and needs are always found to be their correlatives. It is important, he suggests, to note that any theory of need which tries to adjust the social order to the 'anomie of desire' risks forging a new repression. This is clear in the case of sexual repression, since if an adequate theoretical check is not in place the problem will be dealt with as a set of discrete activities (individual problems of performance, perversion, consumption) and not in terms of the structure of desire. Therefore much of what passes for leisure is actually of the same type -- discrete pleasures and activities which then function as signs of an absent totality, and as such are a structure of repressed leisure. Marcuse is right to suggest that apparent frustrations are assuaged.

But what is required, he says in a passage of some interest in the light of his later critique of this idea as still trapped within the perspective of the law as opposed to that of the rule, is a different conception of needs, a perspective which bonds the pleasure principle not to transcendence but to transgression, since all speculation on the nature of basic needs becomes pious. Only desire in all its unpredictable and irrational force, in its heretical and insurrectional surge towards totalization can offer the basis for revolutionary perspectives (Baudrillard 1969a: 7). There can be little doubt that the analysis in *The Object System*, which elaborates a theory of a new order of domestic ambience *where the object system is more coherent than the human system*, is an attempt to work out a theory parallel to that of Marcuse, a theory of the paradox of the liberation of affluence, a site of a new bonding in the repressive order as a whole.

SEMIOLOGY

But apart from Marcuse there is another influence, for the concept of the 'object' which is crucial to Baudrillard is clearly of Barthean inspiration, a 'critical structuralism'. Baudrillard's subsumption of 'furniture' into the category of the object, followed Barthes who had suggested this in his essay on *Elements of Semiology* first published in 1964. In that work Barthes draws the distinction between the 'object' and social 'fact' (Durkheim). In the case of the technical order of the car, he emphasizes, the syntax is very limited or elementary, the scope of the 'speech' of the system very narrow (1967a: 29); in this case it is the social fact, the usage of cars, which has the greater degree of freedom. Furniture also makes up a system:

the language is formed by the oppositions of functionally identical pieces (two types of wardrobe two types of bed, etc.) each of which, according to its 'style', refers to a different meaning, and by the rules of association of the different units at the level of the room ('furnishing'); the 'speech' is here formed either by the insignificant variations which the user can introduce into one unit (by tinkering with one element, for instance), or by freedom in associating pieces of furniture together.

(Barthes 1967a: 29–30)

This leads Barthes to establish a classification from which he compares the garment system and syntagm with the furniture system and syntagm. Thus the system contains the elements (items of clothing, pieces of furniture), the syntagm contains the juxta-positions (shoes—trousers—jacket—hat; or chair—table—wardrobe) (1967a: 63). Barthes himself published a full-scale study of the 'fashion system' in 1967, Baudrillard's study of domestic objects was published in 1968.

Naturally it is tempting to read Baudrillard's work *The Object System* as an application of principles derived directly from Barthes, and indeed Baudrillard invites the reader to do just this. He begins the book by asking how it is possible to classify objects, an activity Barthes had suggested fundamental (1967a: 96). And Baudrillard discusses the possibility of classifying objects from the point of view of technological criteria, but quickly concludes that this would not be useful in the case of everyday objects. Social constraints on the object continually disrupt technological logic (Baudrillard 1968: 12). What interests Baudrillard is the relation between the rational technical system and the apparent 'irrationality of needs' of human beings, and how this contradiction gives rise to ever new needs. Take for example, he says, the simple coffee grinder. The essential components seem to be the (objective) tech-nology, its electric motor, for example. The apparently inessential elements seem to relate to features of its design (shape and colour) which appear highly subjective. This subjectivity, even individual-ized or personalized, is a 'formal connotation' (another Barthesian expression), articulated on this inessential aspect. The difference between craft and industrialized production is that the 'inessential' itself becomes systemized into the latter form, and is relative to its specific market. From the point of method, however, there is major difference between the analysis of language and that of objects. The technological level (the techneme) does not have the same degree of autonomy or stability as the parallel element at the level of meaning (the moneme or phoneme which produce meaning only in combination): the technical level is in constant revolution (1968: 14), and, further, the technical system, unlike a language, is funda-mentally dependent on conditions which are strictly social.

Baudrillard thus begins by making semiological distinctions, and draws parallels directly with the analysis of language. This is not done in a heavy-handed and laboured way, many of the key termino-logical points are made in footnotes. But a great deal hinges on these terms and their meaning. So it is necessary here to clarify them as far as possible. For example, in investigating this important intro-duction to *The Object System* (1968: 7—16), it is clear that Barthes' terminology plays a key role in the way that Baudrillard's argument takes shape. Between the distinction – system of practices/technical system and that of speech/sound elements – there are parallels which suggest a 'profound analogy' between Barthes' term 'field of dispersion' (Barthes 1967a: 84) and Baudrillard's notion of 'marginal difference' (Baudrillard 1968: 15).[3]

Barthes defines the 'dispersal field' as follows: it is constituted by the 'varieties in execution of a unit' as long as these varieties do not pass the threshold of meaning (if the varieties pass this threshold they then belong to another order altogether, as 'relevant or pertinent variations'). To take an alimentary example, the question would relate to the possible variations of a particular dish while it remained recognizably itself. In the car system the term is not so important, as the elements formed at the level parallel to that of *la langue* are more important.

Second, Barthes identifies another concept: the varieties which make up the field are called 'combinative variants'. Barthes notes that, previously considered part of speech (*parole*), they are now held to belong to *la langue*. For example, pronunciation differences have no effect in their function in communicating a direct meaning (denotation), but can be highly significant at a level of connotation: they can indicate a regional accent (1967a: 85). These, like the idea of 'marginal differences' in the object system, appear to act only on the inessential aspects of the phenomenon; however, as with the language system when marginal differences are introduced at the level of the object, the technical system is not indifferent in this way. It is not like phonemic elements; the difference here makes itself felt throughout the whole system, in the 'differential subjectivity of the cultural system which reacts back on the technical order' (Baudrillard 1968: 16).

Thus we see here both an approximation to the project developed by Barthes and a specifically measured distancing. As we look more closely at Baudrillard's relation to Barthes these differences become significant and Baudrillard's methods and objectives, indeed basic terminology, depart radically from those of Barthesian structuralism. Throughout this important theoretical discussion, he uses not only Barthesian terms but also other key terms, especially terms drawn from Sartre relating to the lived experience of social contradictions *vis-à-vis* the object. He suggests that the systematicity of the technological order is not encountered as a lived phenomenon (1968: 11), but that the object is (1968: 12). Significantly it is the inessential aspects which are lived and experienced directly. Indeed, Baudrillard suggests that

> At the technological level there is no contradiction . . . but a human science can only be that of sense and countersense . . . not of an abstract coherence but of lived contradictions in the object system.
>
> (1968: 15)

If we turn to Baudrillard's final concluding chapter where he returns to these themes, we see that his thought has become more complex. Here he compares the traditional or primitive object-symbol with the modern object of consumption. The 'traditional object', and here he turns to the vocabulary of another structuralist, Lévi-Strauss (1961 [1969]: 85), is 'heavy' with connotations, remains interior to human society, and is therefore never actually 'consumed'. The modern object has become external to such social relations and, in receiving its meaning in the context of a system of object-signs, may become part of a system dominated by marginal differences, or systems of pre-structured personalization. Consumption, therefore, assumes significance in modern societies in terms of signs and their systemic articulations; indeed, consumption must be conceived as the consumption not of material objects but of the ideal elements of this differential system. What is consumed is thus a denegated human relationship, 'signified yet absent'. In the last analysis the object is not the focus of a 'lived relationship'; this has become 'abstracted and annulled'.

This conclusion is obviously highly significant, and its elements and implications need to be carefully considered. Consumption is a category which can be applied only to the advanced societies, and in these it is the order of production which orchestrates the position of the object in social relations. Production draws the 'contradictory lived relation' of the object into a repressive integration of a system of 'personalised differences' (1988b: 22). Baudrillard has here fused a number of theoretical traditions: of Sartre, of Barthes and Lévi-Strauss, and of Althusser. The elements can be specified: the emphasis on the lived experience (Sartre), contradiction and determination by production (Althusser), theory of the object (Barthes and Lévi-Strauss). The major emphasis in the work of Barthes is an attack on the petit bourgeois status of myth and object, and on the way that ideology functions to naturalize certain social relations. Baudrillard, on the other hand, clearly wishes to grasp something of a major displacement occurring in the heart of capitalist society, determined by capitalist production itself. Capitalist society, under the impress of the permanent techno-logical revolution and the penetration of relations by the com-modity form, has been able to 'annul' the contradiction between market distribution and essential human needs. Capitalism has in effect been able to act on need, and in a sense has been able to produce human needs as an effect of its system of production. The crucial, explosive, 'lived' contradiction between need and capitalist distribution has been displaced into the abstract sphere of object-signs, which have themselves become important instruments in the mechanisms of class-stratified reproduction in capitalist society.

AMBIENCE

The expositional order of *The Object System* is also formally marked by the influence of Barthes' semiology. Its first two sections investigate the objective functional system of objects and their 'subjective' system, then the fascination of gadgets and robotics, and finally, the socio-ideological system of objects and consumption. It is thus important to be clear about the overall argument of the book. The first two sections attempt to analyse, first, changes in practices of interior design starting from the point of view of the arrangement of furniture and of interior 'ambience', then the 'antique' and other special collections. The third section is concerns the 'meta-system' and the 'dysfunctional' system. This section, though short, has a valuable statement as a recapitulation of the main themes of the book, which explicitly draws on the ideas of Barthes and shows how they were put to work.

This statement suggests that, after analysing objects in their objective forms (the new functional forms of interior layout, and ambience) and their 'subjective' forms (the collection), the book then turns to consider the field of their connotations (Baudrillard 1968: 131). With technological connotations (the degree of perfection of the machine is given by its approximation to perfect automation, which often becomes obsessional and eccentric (a dys-functionality) in gadgetry and meta-functionality in complete robotization). With social connotations: i) the model and the series (like the car), which Baudrillard analyses as systems of marginal differences which personalize objects for an impersonal market; (ii) credit which becomes increasingly important and lived as a form of liberation diffuses the contradictions between production and consumption; (iii) advertising, regarded here as a discourse on objects – a 'pure' inessential connotation – which too is consumed (1968: 205). The end result, in the social system, is a 'tower of Babel' of different levels of signification in which the object system itself lacks a 'true syntax', is 'reduced . . . to an immense combinatorial matrix of types and models, where incoherent needs are distributed without any reciprocal structuration occurring' (1988b: 15).

Thus, although Baudrillard makes use of Barthes, it can now be seen just how different his work is. There is no long methodological reflection (Barthes' *Fashion System* (1985) has fifty pages on method), a limited technical vocabulary (merely the phrases about marginal differences), and at this juncture the argument is placed in a more orthodox framework of the Marxist conception of a capitalist society whose cultural practices are orchestrated by production processes. Baudrillard has, like Barthes, followed an unorthodox way into Marxist theory, parallel to the emphasis of the Frankfurt School, by concentrating almost exclusively on the moment of consumption in the circuits of capital. This is evident in the very specification of the 'object', as opposed to the 'commodity', a term which Baudrillard, like Barthes, resolutely avoids, and for important theoretical reasons. Similarly, his approach is aimed to avoid conventional kinds of criticism of mass production that is criticism made from the point of view of an authentic experience (1968: 46–7). The question as posed by Baudrillard is more interesting: in what way is the meaning or sense of objects themselves changed? (But the obvious temptation, which the term commodity obviates, is the escalation of the processes analysed to all spheres of society and culture without distinction.)

For Baudrillard, what the new system offers appears to be a new 'freedom' (and already at this period the term has a pejorative ring), an emancipation, a liberation for interior design and a new experience, a new ambience, since the traditional milieu with its limited, univocal relation of object, place, and function is broken down (1968: 23–6). Even the physical layout of rooms is significantly altered and connected in new ways with a new diffuseness and mobility. This functional interconnectedness can be thought of as a new order of 'functionality', implying, in turn, a new functionality in the subject, surrounded now not by the simple orifices of traditional windows, but by windows which act on and interact with and modify interior spaces. New lighting systems and new materials seem to make the interior (as object) less substantial. The fixed point of the wall mirror disappears, as does the family portrait and marriage photo: all that which previously acted as a diachronic mirror of the family itself disappears in a new stage of modernity (1968: 28). The paintings and other art works lose their individual value, and are repositioned in the new designed totality – which is also totally designed. Not least, the grandfather clock (a fact also noted by Henri Lefebvre), the temporal equivalent of the mirror in space and 'paradoxical symbol of permanence', has gone.

Again, following Barthes' note that perhaps the time has come for the mythology of the vehicle, the car, to give way to one of driving, of performance, Baudrillard suggests that, for the sociologist, in the light of the change in the mode of existence of objects, the 'sociology of furniture' will give way to a 'sociology of design'. The solid existence of individual pieces of furniture gives way to a new abstraction, which appears, in return, paradoxically, to impoverish each individual piece taken separately. A new kind of homogeneity is the condition of interfunctionality. At the same time advertising reflects this change by calling into existence the consumer as manipulator and arranger. In a sense, he notes, this is pure hype since any individual acts only on the overall space and cannot create an individual decor, as such, in the traditional sense.

Thus a new kind of personality is brought into existence: the designer. But this praxis is completely external to the new system: it does not act as proprietor, or as simple user or enjoyer of these goods, it simply carries a certain responsibility for them. The modern consumer then does not 'consume' objects in the conventional sense of the word: he or she controls them and commands them in their new order. Indeed, advertising even tends to suggest that in such a modern system the individual, in the last resort, does not fundamentally need objects, he or she is only required to act as a kind of technician.

Baudrillard thus elaborates a theory of a basic transformation of the social meaning of objects. In the traditional system, form is the absolute demarcation of interior from exterior. Any container is in a fundamental sense a fixed form, and substance can be said to be in its form. Objects, here furniture in particular, have the primordial function of being material containers, beyond practical function. They reflect a meaning of the world and are part of a complete world of transcendent substances. The house or home is always symbolic of the human body itself; the object is always anthropomorphized in poetic or metaphoric symbolism. The basic order revolves round the meaning ascribed to nature, which, through the fabrication of objects, is transubstantialized. The created world is established through a long filiation of substances, of form on form. This order has now been destroyed, and with it the age-old formal limits of the inside and the outside; *the complex dialectic of being and appearance has been displaced.* The project of modern technicism puts Genesis into question, since origins are cancelled, as are all the old dense, heavy 'essences' of the domestic milieu. The new forms of computation and calculation rest on a new, and total, abstraction of a completely produced world, a world mastered in all respects (1968: 33–5). Baudrillard stigmatizes the new order as 'above all a sublimated anal aggressivity in the game, discourse, classification, distribution' (1968: 35). And, where previously there were obsessions with the moral order of place and cleanliness, in the new system there is a 'kind of cerebral hypochondria of the cybernetician, obsessed with the absolute circulation of messages' (1968: 36). In this new spatial system everything communicates with everything else in a perfectly transparent way. It is the end of mystery, of the secret of initiation.

Baudrillard begins to flesh out the details of the new order of ambience. An important place in the discussion is given to the evolution of colours.[4] He suggests three phases of development. First, traditionally, colours are so strictly circumscribed by form that they really have no independent value, their meanings are symbolic and arrive, always, from the outside. The use of colours in traditional bourgeois interiors is often only as an additional nuance to the already given heavy colour-substance of particular pieces. If the colours are too spectacular the very existence of the 'interior' is threatened. Second, colours have been liberated in their own right only very late in the evolution of such modern objects as vehicles and typewriters: these remained black for a long period. It was the world of painting which first liberated colours, but it took a long time for this liberation to enter into everyday life itself. Now, however, we have bright red furniture, mauve underwear, and these changes are not autonomous, or without problems, for there develops here a virtual 'obscenity of colour' that modernity reduces to the level of interfunctionality of ambience. Bright colours are soon regarded as too aggressive and vulgar and there is a certain return to the 'natural' colours in the higher class one-off models. In mass-produced serial goods bright colours are lived as an emancipation, yet even here too there is a move to compromise into the pastel shades. So black retains its value of conferring 'distinction', and white still dominates in certain good (bath, linen, kitchen) where the body is placed in a border or liminal zone. Here colour makes its gradual appearance only against stiff opposition. Third, today there is a new stage, one in which colours have begun to find a new value, completely determined by the qualities of abstract ambience itself. It seems, Baudrillard suggests, that colour schemes begin to efface themselves qua colour and become integrated combinatorial tonal systems, where colour as such begins to disappear. Separated from form, colours begin to have significance on another axis, that is, as hot or cold, and they are even represented as rhythms. Thus a new mode of calculation is demanded in relation to this new objective tonality.

Such an analysis is, throughout, inspired by, and also subverts, the work of Barthes. And this is true too for the analysis of the transformation of materials themselves. This begins with the disappearance of wood. Barthes himself had written on this in an essay on toys arguing that the modern system of toys no longer allows the child a role as creator, the role ascribed being that of user, a function which accompanies the change of substance:

> plastic material . . . has an appearance at once gross and hygienic, it destroys all pleasure, the sweetness, the humanity of touch. A sign which fills one with consternation is the gradual disappearance of wood, in spite of its being an ideal material because of its firmness and its softness, and the natural warmth of its touch. . . . It is a familiar and poetic substance, which does not sever the child from close contact with the tree, the table, the floor . . . wood makes essential objects, objects for all time. . . . Henceforth, toys are chemical in substance and colour; their very material introduces one to a coenaesthesis of use, not pleasure. These toys die in fact very quickly, and once dead, they have no posthumous life for the child.
>
> (Barthes 1972: 54–5)

This very rich passage should be compared with one by Baudrillard, for whom

> wood draws its substance from the earth, it lives, it breathes, it 'works'. It has latent warmth . . . it keeps time in its fibres, it is the ideal container . . . wood has its own odour, it ages, and it

even has its parasites. . . . In brief this material has a being.
(1968: 45)

But, even so, here Baudrillard begins to depart, again, from Barthes. It is not simply a question of nostalgia, or even the critique of the artificial nostalgia of synthetic materials which produce a 'pseudo-nature'. Something happens in the new ambient order that makes the contrast between natural and unnatural irrelevant. Whether the material is plastic or concrete, the new order is disengaged, and its symbolism is polymorphic. The fundamental issue is no longer the quality of the presence of the object itself, but the value of the item in the ambient harmony of signs; for example, it becomes a question of the abstract meaning of 'oak' or 'teak' in the domestic design, not whether it is real or synthetic 'teak'.

The new interior restructures space, since pieces of furniture become mobile elements in a decentred environent, governed by an abstract system of relations. Colour and material enter this logic not as concrete but as abstract terms open to mental manipulation. These terms are not yet signs, they become signs as they enter into the system. This new order, and its coherence, is not to be confused with 'taste'. It is rather a new order of culture, a new combinatory, irreversible and, in principle, internally infinite: 'no object can escape it just as no product escapes the formal logic of the commodity' (1968: 49). But one material, he reflects, seems almost perfectly suited to the new order: glass. It is without odour, colour, it does not live, it does not die, it may even symbolize abstraction. It is perfect since it also tends to abolish the mysteries of interiority: it is the crystal which permits us to see other worlds. It seems, above all, to materialize abstract space into an ambiguity: it is both close to us and yet far, intimate, and remote, it communicates yet it refuses communication. Take the glass window: here there is transparency without possibility of passage. The shop window allows vision but prohibits touch, it entices yet excludes. Like the structure of ambience, glass interposes itself in its transparency, in its abstraction, between need and object. This material can then be lived as a new liberation, indeed as a new intensified interpenetration of interior and exterior, a new transparency and visibility, a new purity, yet (with its connotations of hygiene and prophylactic) it does not facilitate a genuine opening on to the world while it abolishes its mysteries.

What then happens, Baudrillard asks in a mode of questioning which will disappear from his writing not long after *The Object System*, to the human subject? If, in the new system the free movement of elements is ultimately governed by abstract principles, what happens to the consumer? At this point it is possible, says Baudrillard, to see that the order of lived experience is quite different from social system contradiction. Take sofas, for example. The last thing advertising mentions about them is what they are like to sit on. What counts is rather their positioning, yet the effect of this is that interaction is quite transformed since no one is any longer face-to-face. Even sitting has changed along with all the visceral functions. Previously the bed was heavy with symbolism and meaning, now there is the sofa-bed, settee, divan, etc.; the kitchen, too, has become a laboratory. The idea of function has been transformed into a systematic abstract culturalization: the domain of domestic labour is transformed in relation to a new technical regime of controls. Muscular effort is gradually displaced by other energy systems under cybernetic control, often remote.

In such a world, says Baudrillard, everything has to be 'handy' and easy to operate, the actions of the body beyond the hand, which increase in value, are drastically reduced, and appear to become the accomplice of the new object system in its functioning. But herein lies a felt lack, the absence of previous symbolic structures, and this is compensated for by new 'lines' of advertising which dress up the object into fluid, transitive, enveloping appearances: 'the universal transitivity of forms', whereby, modern civilization 'attempts to compensate for the effacement of the symbolic relation bonded to the traditional bodily regime of work, to compensate for the irreality, the symbolic void of our new power' (1968: 66). Previously, the meaning of the bodily regime of labour was 'overdetermined' by sexual imagery, its rhythms, its exchanges, its resistances. Today all this has changed: against the 'theatre of cruelty' of ancient objects is the prophylactic whitewash and plastic perfection of the new object. The body is no longer a symbolic formation, it is simply connoted by new functions. A new void is ·created where, before such objects, the body once existed, and so the daily ritual order is also ruptured, and are all rituals connected with bodily cycles and natural cycles. Objects appear to become more complicated in relation to the now more simplified, or, rather, less differentiated, human beings who are supposed to be in control. There is a fatal logic in the quest of technology to produce a 'mimesis' of the natural world. If the simulacrum is so well simulated, reality is effaced and man becomes an abstraction (a view also expressed by Lewis Mumford: man is reduced to incoherence by the very coherence of his own constructions (cited in Baudrillard 1968: 69)). Thus the irony of the regression of the human being in the face of technical progress, open, says Baudrillard, to all the new myths of perfect, omnipotent functional objects.

The inevitable logic of the new order is the production of compensatory reaction, a 'mental dynamic, a simulacrum of a lost symbolic relation . . . trying to reinvent a purpose through the force of signs' (1968: 70–1). Baudrillard takes as his example a publicity campaign to sell a cigarette lighter in the form of a beach pebble. It is not advertised on the basis of any superiority of its function as lighter. Its new 'functionality' lies in its fit to the hand, in its being 'handy'. The pebble fits the palm beautifully, indeed the publicity stresses that it is the sea itself which has polished the stone so that it can fit so comfortably in the hand, to be manipulated by man. The connotation is two-fold, says Baudrillard. There is in this industrially produced object an attempt to signify a recovery of the qualities of the craft object, the direct extension of the human body and the object in hand. And the allusion to the sea reproduces the myth of nature in the service of humanity, adapting itself to his least desire. In this myth nature is transformed into culture – the role of polisher, a sublime artisan. This ancient mythological structure is thus combined with craft purpose in a 'miraculous flint': from the sea it is brought to fire.

Again, stimulated by Barthes' writing on cars, Baudrillard devotes considerable time to this subject, where again his analysis diverges from that of Barthes. In the 1950s and 1960s the body of the car was designed as a triumph of speed, often in the form of an aircraft or with overtones of sharks' fins or of birds' wings. This is not a direct connotation of nature, it is argued; rather, it is the attempt to naturalize the object. It is the reign of allegory, and it is in allegory that the modern unconscious begins to speak in a regressive modern fantasy of wings. These wings do not produce any actual speed; it is not an active technical process but a cultural 'pleasure in effigy', the degradation of pure energy into the sign: on the one side a cruel phallic symbolism, a 'simulacrum of power' (for the real power of the car is hidden), and on the other a regression to a narcissistic envelopment of the object.

Baudrillard concludes that these new forms (whether naturalized or not) intervene in the very lived existence of the object itself, as revealed in the content of advertising discourse. The vocabulary of advertising refers constantly to sincerity, warmth, etc., but these provide only a 'false solution to the contradictory mode in which the object lives' (1968: 75), for, in effect, the explosive nature of drives, of desire, is always disavowed. In this way the specific hypocrisy of the new order is surely exposed: whereas in the previous traditional system there was an attempt to compensate for the cruel theatre of the world in an attempt to romanticize nature, to 'hide its obscenity', here there is an attempt to produce an 'inoffensive naturality of signs'. This allows Baudrillard to compare the traditional and modern systems across a number of dimensions: in the traditional system the basic fact of the object is primary, as is the vivid existence of primary human drives and needs. The symbolic order established a 'natural' order of relations between objects and human drives and needs. The modern order establishes an indirect link, a 'cultural' order of manipulable abstractions, between object and human drives, *breaking the order of symbolism*. In the new order nature appears completely mastered: the human subject appears its master. But, in so producing this new order, the new culturality disavows its own nature, conceals from view its actual, dramatic fundamental loss of human reality and power.

THE THEORETICAL PROBLEMS OF *THE OBJECT SYSTEM*

In conclusion it is important to assess the nature and success of the analyses in *The Object System,* for it is clear that this work inaugurates a programme of work which has always remained in touch with its initial vision and purpose. There seem to be a number of very basic problems with the analysis undertaken, about which it is certain Baudrillard himself was fully aware. The first concerns the semiological finery taken from Roland Barthes, and the precise status of Barthes' own analyses which here often act as exemplars. I have already noted the many differences between Baudrillard and Barthes, one of which is the fact that explicit semiological theory plays a minor role for Baudrillard in terms of the manifest content of the text. I also suggest that the semiological trappings are more or less completely redundant, or that their effects could be rendered much more directly by less elaborate means.

What, for example, is the precise role of semiological theory?

Evidently we learn that the object system comes to operate as a system of signs, and that it is the sign, in its system, which is consumed. Yet, perhaps mercifully, we are never presented with a formal analysis of this system. What Baudrillard does, it seems, is to use these terms evocatively: the ambient system is presented only through a large number of thumbnail sketches, or vignettes, of the typical way in which the system operates, on materials, colours, lighting. These descriptive accounts, written with style and wit, do not reveal the action of a rigorous system of analytic concepts. Rather, they demonstrate the specific phenomenal realization of functions. In the end the semiological system works for Baudrillard as a set of manifest rhetorical classifications or categories which are at work in the ordering of material in the study as a whole. And, in this particular work, it is probably true to say that one of the specific results of this is the latent action of Marxist social analysis. This has led some commentators to distance themselves from this work, in the style of Bourdieu:

> One has only to recall that appropriated objects, of all sorts, are objectified social (class) relations in order to see how one might be able to develop a sociology of the world of objects that would be something other than the record of a projective test masquerading as a phenomenologico-semiological analysis (I am thinking of J. Baudrillard, *The System of Objects*.)
>
> (Bourdieu 1984: 567)

This particular comment is, I think, not as clear as it might first appear. First, of course, to see objects as 'class projections' tends in the direction of a certain kind of phenomenology, but many variations are possible, even in Marxism (ironically, Bourdieu's own analyses often tend to the most vulgar forms of reduction). Baudrillard's analyses do not appear to suffer from reductionism of this type, and perhaps it would be possible to turn this gain against Bourdieu. Baudrillard does not present or 'masquerade' under the guise of phenomenology at all, nor does Barthes. But this is not clear-cut, for Baudrillard's study does in many places appear as a form of social phenomenology of objects. Yet could, for example, the analysis of glass be compared with, say, Sartre's famous analysis of the slimy (Sartre 1957: 604–59)? Sartre's analysis is more formal of course and explicitly poses the question 'what mode of being is symbolized by the slimy?' Yet it is clear that we are on the same terrain, for the slimy is experienced at the liminal as a danger to the maintenance of being, and for Baudrillard it is precisely the role of glass in the new ambient system which symbolizes the new denegated transparency. Sartre's theory of the relation to the object is, of course, quite different from Baudrillard's, for it is centred on the relation of the object in a primordial sense to the individual experience (1957: 575–99). The impact of semiology, as in Barthes, is to re-situate the problem as sociological. But instead of the specific analysis being done in terms of the emergence of a defined environment of the signifier, what is presented is an account of the object (or material) as it is experienced, here by both Barthes and Baudrillard as a loss of the enchantment of a previous age, the symbolic order, or of one's childhood in the changing meaning of the 'life and death' of the object.

In this sense the fact that Baudrillard in error changed the very formulation which Barthes presents in *Elements of Semiology* as a key theoretical statement (noted above) is not at all decisive, since the formulation is not followed up in a rigorous way, and is without consequences. Baudrillard, certainly, continues his analysis of the 'marginal differences' between products in a series both in this book and in his next (*Consumer Society*), but nowhere does he attempt closely to define any existing field in which these differences occur, evolve, alter, or in which these differences begin to lose meaning. The idea is an evocative instrument with little semiological analytic power. The analysis does not depend on the principle or the technique of semiological structuralism. Far more important is the analysis of cases by example, the actual analysis of objects: the car, the lighter, the gadget. Even the basic framework of the transition from the traditional form to the modern form is never presented as a rigorous problem of diachrony. What occurs is a scheme for the presentation of a descriptive catalogue of objects in the situation of synchrony, diachrony, and anachrony.[5]

Baudrillard's awareness of this is apparent only in the next work, where he begins by updating, in a dramatic way, the movement towards total ambience in the experience of the modern airport or shopping centre, towards the elimination of the seasons, and explicitly calls this type of analysis a phenomenological one. In that work the analysis moves, he says, to a new level beyond a purely phenomenological description and metaphysical speculation. His analyses very rarely ever again refer to Barthes. The new orientation is towards the strictly anti-phenomenological anthropology of

Lévi-Strauss. Yet even here the actual use of structuralism is only evocative. More and more Baudrillard uses a parallel between the 'structure' of the circulation of messages, or of women, to disengage a specific level of the system of signs which 'structure' and regulate the object system. But, as we shall see, the true effects of structuralist ideas are actually at work in Baudrillard's conception of society itself.

There is one issue however in *The Object System* which was to become important later, and which should not be overlooked. This was picked up again by Baudrillard in an article in 1970 (and also 1972) which recalled his analysis of the psychological analysis of the collection of objects:[6]

> In the collection it is neither the nature of objects nor even their symbolic value that is important; but precisely the sense in which they negate all this, and deny the reality of castration for the subject through the systematic nature of the collective cycle, whose continual shifting from one term to another helps the subject to weave himself a closed an invulnerable world that dissolves all obstacles to the realisation of desire (perverse of course).
>
> (1981b: 93)

It is important to note that from the beginning there was in Baudrillard's project an attempt to elaborate a specific theory of the modern ideological process of fetishization. Whereas others, like Althusser, at this period developed a critique of this notion, and especially the thesis of the fetishism of commodities, Baudrillard sought to theorize the difference between the pathology of the 'golden calf' or treasure, or hoarding as such, and the fetishism of the closed 'systemic' nature of the money system.

This fetishism is not, he argues, an entrapment of the subject in a passion for the object. The new ideological process is:

> the passion for the code, which by governing both objects and subjects, and by subordinating them to itself, delivers them up to abstract manipulation. . . . This is not the fundamental articulation of the ideological process, not in the projection of alienated consciousness into various superstructures, but in the generalisation at all levels of a structural code.
>
> (1981b: 92)

Baudrillard indeed presents this as a decisive criticism of the applicability of the (Sartrean) phenomenological notion of alienation,

> of a force that returns to haunt the individual severed from the product of his labour, and from the marvels of his misappropriated investment (labour and effectiveness). It is rather the (ambivalent) fascination for a form . . . a state of absorption, for better or worse, in the restrictive logic of a system of abstraction. Something like a desire, a perverse desire, the desire of the code is brought to light here . . . just as the perverse psychological structure of the fetish is organised, in the fetish object, around a mark, around the abstraction of the mark that negates, bars and exorcises the difference of the sexes.
>
> (1981b: 92)

In terms of a conception of the evolution of capitalist forms, this is evident in the shift from the simple fetishism of the commodity and of labour, at the period of the dominance of labour processes, to the more generalized form of the labour of signification, the production of sign-values (which perhaps could be called, if care is taken in the definition, a fetishism of the sign-object).

Baudrillard's project then is very specifically a semiological and psychological extension of Marx:

> the collective process of production and reproduction of a code, a system, invested with all the diverted, unbound desire separated out from the real process of real labour and transferred into precisely that which denies the process of real labour. This fetishism is actually attached to the sign object, the object eviscerated of its substance and history, and reduced to the state of marking a difference, epitomising a whole system of differences.
>
> (1981b: 93)

And in this perspective, he argues, two quite different cultural orientations can be identified: first, a complex which is articulated around the forces of desire, negativity, castration, ambivalence, and a symbolic function (eros, death), and, second, a complex, which is dominant in our societies, of need, positive satisfaction, rights to the body, which are organized around semiological functions (differential alternation). This casts a retrospective theoretical glance at *The Object System*, which can in this light be seen as analysis of the ideological process in capitalist societies as a fundamental process, not of class oppression, but of the 'semiological reduction of the symbolic order' (Baudrillard 1981b: 98).

Chapter 4

Technology and culture
Baudrillard's critique of McLuhan and Lefebvre

Baudrillard's thought, like that of Marx or McLuhan, has sometimes been accused of technological determinism, a mode of
analysis which suggests that the fundamental springs of social
change are to be found in the effects of machines, mechanization,
developments in the means of communications (media), which
social relations themselves interact with but ultimately follow.
Baudrillard's reflections on technology were presented in two short
but in some respects surprising essays in 1967 and 1968 (published
as 1969b).

McLUHAN[1]

The first is a reading of Marshall McLuhan, who remains a decisive
influence on Baudrillard, which immediately grasps the scope of the
vision of three great historic periods, actually very similar to the one
developed by Lefebvre and himself at this period: the first, the
period of tribal to feudal society, dominated by cool cultures, then
the period of hot culture, of literature and the book, and the final
period, again cool, the period of the electronic mass media. The
critique of Marx implied here was that his analysis rested simply on
the effect of the machine, which even in his day was, with the
telegraph, already obsolete. The major mechanical revolutions
(even in printing) were only physical extensions of human capacities
and primarily visual in mode of communication, yet they also
involved an element of self-amputation, as capacities were given to
the machine. Literacy has led to the vast increase in mechanization,
specialization, the division of labour, and the industrial revolution,
a process based on linear causality – deriving from the book. With
the electric media all this is fundamentally overthrown, and the

explosive form of book culture is displaced by one that is implosive, cool. Even causality becomes configurational, and the world becomes decentred yet everything is contemporaneous. The end of Euclidean space, and the beginning of feedback. Television is not a continuation of the book, nor an extension of labour and the machine. Electricity and the satellite revoke the process of metropolization and centralization. Culture returns in a new way to a tactile world: iconic and mosaic. Baudrillard notes the irony McLuhan suggests – Third World tactile villagers pass directly into the global village of subtle yet tactile electronic culture. Baudrillard interprets McLuhan as an optimist, since the spectre of conformity is the outcome of the second order which has now passed.

Baudrillard comments: this optimism is based on a misunderstanding of the historical dimensions here, and especially the social history of the media. Even so, McLuhan's analysis is not absurd. The principal fault lies in the 'baroque' notions of 'hot' and 'cool' media (hot being information delivered in high definition with low empathy, cool being low-definition information with intense involvement; for example, the modern game is formal, fascinating, limited in its rule-bound systemic nature). Cool cultures are those of ritual, symbolic festival, dance, and orality. Literacy is hot and rests at a distance, disaggregates action and reaction, and so do radio and television which are only extensions of the book. Baudrillard notes that this proposition is extremely obscure, but that there is an interesting idea, the possibility of a short circuit between the hot and cool; the possibility of a 'brutal introduction of radio into cool oral homogeneous culture' is paralleled by the 'irruption of the television, a cool medium, into the literary and scientific hot culture' of which 'we are far from having measured the consequences' (1967: 224). The argument that television ushers in a cool phase, says Baudrillard, overlooks the fact that there are very different orders of participation, active and passive, not governed by the medium itself; to look at a painting by Vermeer is not the same thing as to look at op art.

But it is easy to misunderstand McLuhan here, says Baudrillard, especially the formula that the medium is the message. When McLuhan argues about the book, and book culture, it is to emphasize that culture is primarily influenced by the constraints of a certain form of systematization. The book is first and foremost an object, and in the long run *it is not the ideas which are carried in books which are important in themselves but the discipline they impose*. It is evident, Baudrillard says in agreement, that the manifest content of media tends to hide their function: take the railways – it is not any particular journey that counts, but rather the vision of the world that is made possible. It is the same with the television,

> which has precisely the effect of neutralizing the lived and unique character of events which it relays which it makes into a discontinuous 'message', signs interposable with others in the abstract dimension of a television programme.
>
> (1967: 229–30)

Take, for example, the difference between the effect of television in the west and in the Third World. In the former it seems to transmit messages, but in the Third World it transmits the objects that come from the west. From this, says Baudrillard, it can be seen that such media eventually introduce a vast process of homogenization as media relate across cultures and between themselves. This is the 'totalitarian message' of the consumer society.

But the weakness of McLuhan's understanding of history means, says Baudrillard, that his optimism is misplaced. For behind the new media lies the persistent recrudescence of imperialism, nationalism, and feudalist bureaucracies. Even if the new media are in his terms the extensions of the central nervous system, they are still invested with the structures of power and regressive fantasy. So, although 'his book is brilliant and fragile, it lacks the historical and social dimension which would make it something other than a mythological "travelling" of cultures and their destinies' (1967: 230).

LEFEBVRE[2]

This important rejection of technologism in favour of a social and cultural analysis of technology was followed by a second essay which attacked Lefebvre's notion of the liberation of technology in order to serve the people. This idea is based on crucial misunderstandings, he argues. The 'emancipation' of technology in the Industrial Revolution was not the liberation of a pure force, but one that had evolved under the control of previous ruling political and military groups, as an instrument of domination and discrimination. When these forces escaped the control of corporations they entered into social mythology as a resource open to all, innocent and distinct from political process. Technology is not only an instrument for the domination of nature, it is an instrument of social mastery, both in a directly political but also in a more complex way as differential acculturation. It is this second process which works against the process of levelling and homogenization, for it establishes a level of discrimination in the educational system (technical education is, in the west, an inferior formation; in eastern Europe there is an exaltation of technology but in a directly utilitarian mode).

There is also a huge internal dislocation between the levels and qualities of technology itself, between theoretical and high-status technology and the common, practical, even domestic forms, and this is reproduced by a hierarchy of social distinctions in levels of culture, so that huge portions of society have a connection with technology only through its myths. Rising social groups encounter it in self-help programmes, that is, a second-class form of technical learning, suitable for the scientifically uneducated which functions to legitimate the actual social structures of power. Thus the remarkable ambiguity of technology can be seen in the fact that everywhere it is all powerful, yet at the same time it occupies a shameful position in culture. The myths of the everyday, banal use of technology remain trapped in infantile states of development, where everything seems to come from High Technology: it is 'reified in consumption' (Baudrillard 1969b: 151). In fact, there is only a single, complex, contradictory whole, since there is no longer a High Culture of which the mass culture is a 'fallen' form (according to a scheme of the higher model and the common series) for both 'obey the same logic' (1969b: 152). Both are mutually dependent, and the result is that everyday life is thrown into a state of permanent underdevelopment. What happens is the appearance of the heroic high tech forms (space, nuclear power) into the mythology of domestic gadgetry. These are not lived as 'fallen' but are transfigured into signs of and promise of total technological revolution. Everyday items then come to function as myth, as supports for the idea of technological transcendence beyond social contradiction. The car and the space-ship are two poles of an ideological field, and redouble themselves in a system where each serves the imaginary of the other. Thus they are already, in their structures and functions, mediated by an ideology of social division, discrimination, and hierarchy.

In effect, objects are not lived as rational and practical innovations, but as erratic novelties, their fascinations formed in relation to established myths of promise and danger. They are received in a society in which technology is liberated, precisely as objects, that is to say, fixed and idealized as avant-garde signs, inhabiting an unreal everyday life. This form of consumption tends to be more and more an aesthetic one, related to science fiction and simulation, founded on a form of consumption with marked social hierarchy and privilege. Thus Baudrillard arrives at Lefebvre's slogan 'all technology to the service of everyday life' (see Lefebvre, 1971: 206) as itself based on false notions of the innocent and pure nature of technology and its promise of social salvation. A revolution of the kind Lefebvre hopes to achieve could not be achieved through the application of current technology to social life. If there is a potential in technology, it will already have had to be transformed itself as a social practice. The suggestion that technology is a rational principle which can be used to overthrow an irrational superstructure overlooks, Baudrillard argues, the decisive fact that *technology is already structured by social and cultural privilege and discrimination.* It is modern society itself which invents technology as its principle of salvation, but this is a strategy of power itself. His concluding passage is highly revealing on the nature of Baudrillard's ideological and cultural background assumptions at this stage of his theorizing:

> In order that technical innovation inaugurate true structural changes, it is necessary first of all to install a technical culture, that is to say the slow and difficult substitution of traditional culture by another system of values, and to install a radically different educational system, not so much in its content as in its apprenticeship forms. It is necessary to escape from the Spectacle of Technology, and of the Myth which sustains it, in order to realize the principle of 'rational capacity and its exercise', and to carry this principle to the roots of social apprenticeship if there is to be an end to magical manipulation.
>
> (1969b: 155)

Chapter 5

The rigours of consumer society

Give him such economic prosperity that he will have nothing left to do but to sleep

Dostoevsky

THE PROBLEM

It is in Baudrillard's major sociological work, *Consumer Society* (1970) that the immense vistas of his sociology become visible, and the problems dealt with in the earlier book are situated in a more general theory. It is true that the writing of the *Consumer Society* develops without a formal structuralist apparatus, and there is no appeal to the semiological niceties of Roland Barthes. This text is written in a more accessible and modest way, yet its analyses have a lucid and brilliant character. Many commentators have suggested that this is Baudrillard's most successful effort, yet despite its very directness very few have grasped its true theoretical force and originality. Thus it is somewhat ironic that, while many other moderate works of Parisian social theory of this period have been translated into English, this one, still popular in France, has been ignored. Parts of it, however, are now included in English translations in collections of Baudrillard's writings, but these translators are replete with errors which arise from a lack of familiarity with the theoretical terminologies on which Baudrillard draws.

Unfortunately a recent, rare discussion of this particular essay by Baudrillard, by Kellner, is somewhat typical in this respect. In so far as Kellner works towards a critical rejection of Baudrillard's contribution, it is important to assess the extent to which the criticisms are genuinely aimed at Baudrillard rather than at a construction made out of mistranslation and misunderstanding. For

Kellner, for example, the main point of the book (he says in a comment inserted between quotations for which it is difficult to find any principle of selection) is the idea that 'commodities are part of a system of objects correlated with a system of needs', where the words 'system' and 'system of needs' are underlined, as if to emphasize something in the words which contradicts Baudrillard's formulation, which says the opposite (Kellner 1989a: 13). Or again, it is suggested that 'consumption becomes the centre of life', where the word consumption is underlined. Or again, 'in this society, consumption of commodities signifies happiness' – yet a few lines later Kellner tells us, quite to the contrary, that for Baudrillard 'consumption is not to interpreted primarily in relation to pleasure'. Briefly and cavalierly dismissing its theory, Kellner ends by criticizing the position developed because its does not have a 'theory of class or group revolt', a comment which follows closely his observation that 'Baudrillard points to contemporary manifestations of irrational violence . . . which he interprets as a kind of social revolt', and he quotes Baudrillard on the movement of May 1968 to the effect that it can be understood only as a transformation of an apparently disaffected mass into an active force, meaning, he insists, that this potentiality was already present (Kellner 1989a: 18). Kellner approaches this work in a way which is content to remain at one remove from it. Astonishingly, he reaches the conclusion that perhaps it takes 'Frankfurt School theory . . . to a higher level' (Kellner 1989a: 19).

A very different reading is, however, not only possible but demanded if Baudrillard's whole project is to be grasped, for Kellner is undoubtedly correct to point to the decisive significance of this work in Baudrillard's writings, for this work is in fact one of the most important contributions to social theory in a period of exceptional theoretical productivity in France. Kellner's unexplicated adherence to the importance of the notion of the human agent and to the theory of revolution (as organized by a revolutionary party) seems to blind him to the specific arguments of the book. And Kellner is not at all alone here, for if this book by Baudrillard is itself a contribution to structural Marxism, commentaries and discussions of structural Marxism have on their side completely ignored this analysis. As recent introductions to Baudrillard's thought of this period are inaccurate or self-contradictory, the meaning and significance of his work are likely to remain opaque, and its potential impact on social theory to be cancelled at the moment it becomes widely available. There is a certain amount of mystery here.

Certainly one of the crucial problems of reading this work is that it probably appears descriptive of a certain state of affairs in modern society.[1] If the book does not have the formal brilliance of philosophical organization of, say, an essay by Althusser, it certainly compensates for this by its real theoretical originality and its new cultural analyses. As Kellner points out, this is Baudrillard's own original encounter with Marxist thought and his most important contribution to it. Indeed Baudrillard sought to quote Marx's observation as a point of departure:

The busiest streets of London are crowded with shops whose showcases display all the riches of the world . . . but all these worldly things bear odious white paper labels with Arabic numbers and then laconic symbols Lsd. This is how commodities are presented in circulation.

(Marx 1971: 87)

In Baudrillard's words, although the objects of the commodity world are the produce of human practice, they have come to surround us in the modern period, not as objects such as Marx's 'Indian shawls, American revolvers, Chinese porcelain, Parisian corsets, furs from Russia and spices from the tropics' (1970: 87) but as those which might be imaged in a 'bad science fiction novel' (1988b: 30). His point of departure is Marx's thesis that in capitalist societies what is produced is produced as a commodity, as something bought and sold on markets. Thus, under capitalist conditions prevailing in the early nineteenth century production was no longer production for a particular consumer. At the same time producers, workers, or labourers, also become commodities on the labour market – or, rather, and this is crucial to Marx's elaboration of a comparative table of labour systems, the labourer sold his labour-power on the market. This process is one which involves a considerable effort of transformation of human relations into relations which are, in decisive respects, relations between objects; they become human relations inflected with commodity attributes. In other words, they become reified, and relations of interpersonal dependency are replaced with those of a far more objective character. As Baudrillard reads this, 'the loss of the human relationship (spontaneous, reciprocal, symbolic) is the most fundamental fact of our societies' (1970: 255).

As we have already seen in the earlier writings of Baudrillard, in approaching the issue of the reification of social relations it is a relatively short transition to a Marxist social phenomenology, and especially a phenomenology of a humanist orientation. This tends to proceed through the analysis of the increasing penetration of social relations by the cash nexus and its subsequent dehumanizing effects on consciousness itself. Just as an analysis of the dehumanization of social relations is achieved with brilliance here, it can paradoxically be aligned with the brusque dismissal of the importance of the appearance of the idea of reification and alienation in the later works of Marx (e.g., by the Althusserians as an ideological version of the alienation of philosophically postulated essences). But it is clear that Marx's later work does continue a specific theme of very basic significance, that of the changing character not only of the lived relation (towards objectivity), but also that fundamental changes in the categories of knowledge and thought are also implied (followed up, of course, by writers like Lukacs, Lefebvre, and Sartre as a *reification of consciousness* in everyday life).

As I mentioned in chapter three Baudrillard himself identified some of his analyses of the object system as phenomenological:

> In the phenomenology of consumption, the general acclimatization of the life, goods, services, behaviours, and social relations represents the perfected, 'consummated' stage of evolution which, through articulated networks of objects, ascends from pure and simple abundance to a complete reconditioning of action and time, and finally in the systematic organization of ambience, which is characteristic of drugstores, shopping malls, or the modern airport − our cities of the future.
>
> (1970: 23−4)

This casts an interesting retrospective light on the essay on *The Object System*, where this kind of analysis prevailed.

But Baudrillard continues this theme in an effort *to go beyond* this kind of analysis:

> The truth about consumption is that it is a function of production and not a function of pleasure, and therefore, like material production, it is not an individual function but one that is directly and totally collective. No theoretical analysis is possible without the reversal of traditional givens: otherwise

. . . we revert to a phenomenology of pleasure.

(1988b: 46)

There can, then, be no mistaking the direction of Baudrillard's project, which is to initiate a quite new kind of analysis in this domain, which he calls a 'theoretical analysis' leading to the introduction of 'theoretical hypotheses' (1988b: 46) in contradistinction to a purely 'ideological analysis'.

THE CONCEPT OF CONSUMPTION

The crucial theoretical discussion however begins with a systematic critique of homo economicus, especially the assumptions which revolve around the notion of the sovereign individual consumer who functions to maximize pleasures in relation to a finite but uncoordinated set of needs. Modern affluent society appears in this perspective to be driven by the full action of individual wants now given complete freedom of action in a situation of great abundance. This general conception, for Baudrillard, is both theoretically unacceptable (the individual appears to want what he needs and needs what he wants), and empirically unable to account for the specific proliferation of goods and objects.[2] Although apparently made up of empirical components, the notion of homo economicus is a metaphysic, and has to be replaced with a more incisive social theory. So too he says in a move which breaks with humanist Marxism, does its alternative, the notion of the alienated consumer, a 'pseudo-philosophy', itself only part of the mythology of consumer society (1970: 100).

Baudrillard proceeds by elaborating his own 'genealogy' of consumption (1988b: 42), indicating four basic departures from traditional economies: a new technical system of machines, capital and rational calculation, a wage system based on abstract labour, and a system of demand related to an integrated system of needs. These 'needs' are radically different from the category of pleasure (*jouissance*), since they are systematically related in their own right, and not, as one might think, a direct connection of want with an object which might in principle satisfy it. In this light, he argues, it is important to consider consumption not as some slight addition to the circuit of capital (an alienation), but as a crucial productive force for capital itself. Thus those who present affluence as a consequence of advertising pure and simple, the fetishism of commodity as pure ideology, or as the result of the expression of inherent needs, only indulge themselves in a form of 'magical thought' or reduction to the diabolic power of the technostructure (1988b: 43). His formulation is that the practice of consumption is 'the most advanced form of the rational systematisation of the productive process at the individual level' (1988b: 43). And it is clear, he says, that what the naïve notion of affluence as the liberation of human desires neglects is the paradoxical reassertion from time to time of puritanical ideologies. The very instance in which the individual realizes his or her own pleasures is in fact the site not only of a new consciousness but, more fundamentally, of new disciplines running parallel to apparent emancipation – disciplines which carry their own forms of systematization, concentration, seduction, gratification, and repressive de-*sublimation* – in other words, he notes, *alienation correctly understood* (1988b: 43).[3]

The presentation of Baudrillard's own position has three basic stages. First, the basic thesis of the essay is that consumer society is a new and unprecedented phase of capitalism. This is already explicit in Baudrillard's genealogy. As his argument develops, it is evident that the new stage is a concentration, a stage of monopolization and a new stage of the organization of credit which is the critical support for new emergent features. Theoretically, consumerism is conceived here not as a cultural logic but as a form of the productive forces of capital:

> credit here plays a determining role, even though it only has a marginal impact on the spending budget. The idea is exemplary. Presented under the guise of gratification, of a facilitated access to affluence, of a hedonistic mentality, and of 'freedom from the old ideas of thrift' etc., credit is in fact the systematic indoctrination of forced economising and an economic calculus for generations of consumers who, in a life of subsistence, would have otherwise escaped the manipulation of demands and would have been unexploitable as a force of consumption.
>
> (1988b: 49)

To claim consumption is a 'function of production' (1988b: 46) is not to say there are no primary needs, but to say that all such needs are socially articulated.

Second, this new consuming mass is disciplined by a new ideological obligation to enter consumption proper. Leaving the field of anomie to the past, modern ideologies pressure the consumer to 'try out' the latest commodities, to enter into the spirit of the latest gadget. An obsessive new curiosity is born here, and it develops in the mass the fear of missing the latest fashion, something new. This structure cannot be recognized by individualist assumptions of the nature of the consumer, for it is a social fact in the primordial sense, yet the social fact is realized in an individual manner, or rather an individualized manner, so that the consuming mass, rather like Saussure's 'speaking mass', has no collective existence.

Third, the essential point is that this social fact cannot be analysed as a direct relation of consumer to the objects of consumption, as this misses the problem. The new system works at the level of a new ideology and a new code (a system of structural differences). Here Baudrillard draws on Saussure and Lévi-Strauss, for whom the elements of such a system are arbitrary: what counts is the set of internal relations in the system (1988b: 47), like the exchange of women in primitive societies forms a code in which the society, as Durkheim puts it, talks to itself. Thus it is possible to say that the ideological forces at work in the object are not donated from subjective desires, but rather they *prestructure* subjective desire. And in the era of monopoly capital the subject, even, is subjected to pre-structured personalization.[4]

CONSUMER SOCIETY

This induces two different tendencies in social life. One is the dramatic reduction of previous demarcations and divisions in society which were previously experienced a social division and contradictions: they now become minor differences (Baudrillard 1970: 126). This is to be explained, he suggests, on the basis that all previous societies were established on the foundation of close personal ties. Today society is more and more characterized by produced social 'relations', which are themselves converted into 'objects' to be consumed. The second tendency is a marked change in relation to the object so that social differentiation is mediated in the object, by the object not the subject. Following Lévi-Strauss, he argues that what occurs is a kind of meta consumption. As differences are structured into objects, it is precisely the *differential social relations which are consumed*.[5] Social status is therefore reproduced principally in the consumption of object differences, and it is at the level, a second, unconscious level, of its inner relations that the code itself functions as an unconscious ideological apparatus (*dispositif*); and it is highly effective as a disciplinary structure because it is desired, pleasurable, gratificatory (1970: 136). It makes its appearance in the form of involved emancipation and free choice, under the power of the individual will, yet the code determines this process effectively, perhaps inducing the deepest form of social control.[6]

But this general process is also intensified by the action of the new mass media. According to Baudrillard, this works through the construction of cultural models, which like the exterior forms of personalization of objects, come to exercise new personalization effects on consumers. His main example here is the catastrophic turn in the form of the masculine and the feminine in consumer society. His argument has three basic steps. First, modern advertising induces a change in the relation to the subject itself, in the general direction of increased narcissism, even a 'personalized narcissism': the ideal 'referent' is the buyer, the purchaser – actually a collective social process which diffracts itself towards each subject as it interpellates them. The system ultimately induces a form of subject auto-seduction: *the self-consumption of the subject*. This is a form of the inner 'calling' of the system induced in the individual. Second, it is exercised most explicitly in relation to women through the formation of models, and this works entirely on the level of collective myths. Here what occurs is a displacement of spontaneous qualities of beauty or charm, for those mediated by a system of signs of beauty. The object consumed by women is a model. Against spontaneous femininity, femininity here becomes 'functional', sophisticated, fashioned. The model provides each woman with a physical personality, a mask. Third, functional femininity corresponds to functional masculinity. The two form a system and the logic of this system originates not in the reality of sexual relations but in the ideological code itself. This implies the existence of at least three levels: first, that of 'real', 'natural' sexuality, which, says Baudrillard, is, in fact, highly arbitrary (for each sex is charged bisexually); second, each of the fundamental historically produced sexual categories being ordered hierarchically (and remaining so, despite some modifications); finally, the level of the system of models, which in many respects reinforces the distinctions of the second level, the social order. There is also, he notes, the possible emergence of a new 'hermaphroditic' model linked to the new adolescent market. The consumer society generalizes the feminine model across the whole field of consumption (1970: 143).

The argument, which this brief account indicates only in broad outline, fuses Marx, Saussure, and Freud into a brilliant theory of a new social formation. The commodity form, fundamental to capitalist exchange, is complemented by a paradoxical alteration in the relations of consumers and products, through, first, the evolution of a sign exchange system (*exploitation and oppression work in the code itself*) and a change in the consumer in the direction of intensified narcissism (*the oppressed consumer mass is cathected to the object and self-consumption*). Baudrillard's contribution here, apart from the formation of this synthesis, is to work towards a concept of personalization through the commodity. He produces his own concepts here on the model of Barthes and the material in *The Object System*. He introduces concepts around the notion of the new basic common denominators: the 'smallest common culture' is that minimal culture demanded in the consumer society (1970: 155), complemented by the 'smallest marginal difference' in style and status, so that *the whole culture becomes a combinatorial machine*. The new culture is not a complex syntax; its basic elements are combined together in multiples such as the structure of the basic question and response survey (1970: 157).[7] The individual is summoned to choose from a range of objects, and a range of questions, and a range of credit companies. This is a *consumer society*.

SYMPTOMATOLOGY

It is possible to see here the emergence of a perspective which in many key respects is very close to, yet distant from, that of Bachelard and Althusser for whom ideological relations are always lived in the form of a misrecognition and the development of scientific knowledge involves revolutionary ruptures of epistemological substructures. This was certainly also the leading idea of French Freudians in this period and it seems to have had a deep impact on Baudrillard's thought.[8] In this particular work Baudrillard utilizes a number of technical terms from Lacanian psychoanalytic theory, and chooses to explain his epistemology by use of parallels with Freudian conceptions of hysteria:

In the hysterical or psychosomatic conversion the symptom, like the sign, is (relatively) arbitrary. Migraine, colitis, lumbago, angina, or generalized fatigue: there is a chain of somatic

signifiers which the symptom 'walks' along – as there is an inter-
linking of object/signs, or object/symbols, along which walk,
not needs . . . but desire, and a further determination, that of
unconscious social logic.

(1970: 107, and see 295–6)

Baudrillard's key propositions refer, then, to displacements and to
a structural field in depth. And, like symptoms, hysterical objects
'obey the same logic of shifts, transference and of apparently
arbitrary convertibility' (1988b: 44, trs. mod.). For Baudrillard the
modern world is thus to be grasped in an analogy with 'generalized
hysteria'. Understanding and reading the world of needs and
objects literally will fall into the traditional error of treating the
symptom only to find another reappearing in a different site.
Another way of approaching the issue is to imagine that there are
two quite different languages, which interpenetrate: the logic of
objects is a vast paradigm 'through which something else speaks'
(1988b: 45). Yet what is spoken from the deeper language is realized
as a 'lack' which cannot be satisfied at the surface. Just as with the
hysteric, 'this evanescence and continual mobility reaches a point
where it becomes impossible to determine the specific objectivity of
needs'. The analysis concludes that between the fluidity of desire
and that of differential significations,

> specific and finite needs only become meaningful as the focus of
> successive conversions. In their substitutions they signify, yet
> simultaneously veil, the true spheres of signification – that of
> lack and that of difference – which overwhelm them from all
> sides.
>
> (1988b: 45 trs. mod.)

Society is thus a complex structure and its present state one of
crisis.

This particular theoretical characterization marks out a number
of key processes. First is the basic notion of the drive, of desire,
and of its correlate, the 'lack'. Many Marxists of this period saw in
Freud's idea of the drive a force which in some critical respects
could be used as the basis of a critique of the ideological circularity
of humanist accounts, for Freud very precisely specified the
primacy of the drive over the object (only on this basis, he argued,
could variations in history be accounted for). Althusser tried to
develop similar ideas in terms of the immanent logic of structural

processes in capitalist society itself, and especially as the basis for reading the theory of mode of production as a structure in which the determinant element was the function of the means of production (thus contrasting the structural theory of practice against that of praxis in which the key term was telos or goal or purpose).

Second, Baudrillard here suggests a particular usage of the Saussurean principle of the arbitrary nature of the signifier, by which he meant the idea that the real object in the world (the referent) has no essential relation to the way in which its sign is formed. Saussure also elaborated a conception of the way in which language functions, not so much by the presence of positive terms themselves, but rather by the elaborate play of abstract differences between them. Derrida, in a famous critical support of Saussure's principle, argued that this breakdown by Saussure could be used as a basic instrument for an attack on the logocentric metaphysics of western philosophical teaching on language. But more than this, Baudrillard has developed these ideas very specifically in the context of an attempt to highlight the substitutability of the symptom in hysteria, i.e., the non-essential nature of the site of the symptom, implying its mobility and its appearance as displacement. Now this idea suggests a complex pattern of effects (at the level of the signifier), but where the signification is always displaced from the signified. In a sense this idea suggests a pathology, since for Saussure it is the absent environment of the term which gives it its overdetermined value. Here, the value of the term (as symptom) is, presumably, always the same.

The third implication is that Baudrillard has adopted or developed his own version of the principle of the *'Darstellung'*, the idea, developed by the Althusserians from Marx's *Capital*, that the ideological forms of commodity relations, the particular structure of commodity fetishism, both reveal and veil the production process as a whole (very much like the process of the metaphoric or the metonymic relation in which representation occurs indirectly).[9] This idea was developed further by Althusser himself in drawing out the difference between the determinant element of a process and the dominant aspect of a process (it is the economy which determines the dominant site of social struggle). To this principle was added the idea that in each dominant site of struggle could be found the main elements of ideological fetishism or mystification: in feudalism, religion; in capitalism, commodity fetishism. Of course this logic could easily be extended, as it is in Baudrillard's case: in the evolution of capitalism such commodity fetishism become the dominant instance could shift the decisive mechanisms towards the object of consumption itself.

Baudrillard does not, however, immediately draw out these implications, but rather is content to state the imagery of generalized hysteria and to move towards an important working principle (which he calls his 'theoretical hypothesis'). His argument rejects the ideological notion of sovereign individual needs and pleasures as the explanatory principle of market processes. On the contrary, it is essential to specify an underlying unconscious causal determination of social forces which comes to the surface in a constrained sphere of (differential) signs. Consumption must seem to be available in such a way as to be exclusively the 'free' pleasure of the individual consumer; but Baudrillard's suggestion is that it is more to the point to think of consumption as founded on the 'denegation' of such pleasure (1988b: 46; 1970: 110, trs. mod.), and as a determined sphere of repressive social constraint.

It is worth recalling the precise meaning of this term 'denegation' for Lacanians and Althusserians. Brewster's glossary of theoretical terms is useful here. The term (*Verneinung*) was used by Freud to

> designate an unconscious denial masked by conscious acceptance, or vice versa . . . it is one of a set of concepts for the place of the conscious system in the total psychic mechanism (the unconscious) which Althusser applies by analogy to the place of ideology in the social formation.
>
> (in Althusser 1970: 312)

Correct translation is thus crucial, and it is unfortunate that the current English translation, and Kellner's usage, accepts only the notion of denegation as simple denial. This renders Baudrillard's theory into a nullity, as it is precisely Baudrillard's aim to make this term a key instrument in the understanding of a consumption process at once rationalized at the individual level, as governed by a perverse pleasure principle, and maintained at the social level by the repressive ideology of consumption itself.

IDEOLOGY AND OVERDETERMINATION

Baudrillard is led therefore, in describing the reign of the sign system, to the use of concepts of a Durkheimian kind, social fact

and social constraint, though his acknowledged source now is not
Durkheim or Barthes, but rather Lévi-Strauss:

That which confers on consumption its character of a social fact
is not derived from that which it apparently draws from nature
(satisfaction, pleasure), it is rather the essential process by which
it separates itself from nature (what defines its code, as institution, as system of organisation).
(1988b: 47; 1970: 110, trs. mod.)

And, just like Durkheim, Baudrillard suggests the new consumer
mythology is a way in which 'our entire society communicates and
speaks of and to itself' (1988b: 48). But there is more to it than a
doubling up of languages; the new mythologies of consumerism are
themselves an immense ideological force which bring into existence
new imperatives. Just as the puritan ideologies enforced a discipine
of saving and economy, he suggests, modern ideologies develop a
paradoxical set of obligations towards expenditure and credit. *The
puritan, as individual, was converted into a kind of enterprise constantly seeking opportunities for investment, the modern individual
becomes an 'enterprise of pleasure and satisfaction'* (1988b: 48).

It is possible to argue, in the vein of Durkheim and Marx, that
the idea of consumption as a domain of anomie or anarchism may
have been true only of an early period or periods of capitalism: it is
no longer a domain without norms, but, quite the contrary, a
domain increasingly subject to a new organization and discipline.
This domain now has its own specific effectivity, its own forms of
regulation and sanction. Indeed, it is possible to argue, he suggests,
that in this way a quite new phenomenon appears, that of the new
consuming mass, just as exploitable as the new working classes
were in the nineteenth century. This kind of analysis depends very
much on the elaboration of a certain kind of conception of the
social structure as complex, in which a series of dramatic and
irreversible displacements have taken place (rather like Freud's
conception of the displacements of zones during sexual maturation,
a key parallel indicated by Balibar (in Althusser and Balibar 1970)),
and in which production still functions as a determinant moment.
This position in epistemology, says Baudrillard, is the only one
which enables the analyst to avoid the perils of empiricism on the
one hand and descriptive metaphysics on the other (1988b: 46).

From the point of view of method, Baudrillard goes on to
develop the implications of his position towards a bifurcation of

perspectives, both of which depart radically from a phenomenology of lived ideologies. He expresses the object as a new form of consumption as a system:

1. dominated by the constraint of signification, at the level of *structural analysis*;
2. dominated by the constraint of production and the cycle of production in *strategic analysis* (socio-economic-political).

(1988b: 51; 1970: 116, trs. mod., emphasis added)

The conception of the society to which these perspectives now relate he indicates as

– a new objective situation governed by the same fundamental process, but overdetermined by a new morality – the whole corresponding to a new sphere of the productive forces in the process of controlled reintegration in the same expanded system.

(1988b: 51)

This formulation is of crucial importance for the arguments in this study, and deserves close consideration.

The appearance of Baudrillard's conception of the social whole has strikingly original features, just as does his idea of the two principal forms of analysis undertaken. Again it is with Althusser that the main comparisons here have to be made, since it was his theoretical interventions that popularized the conception of overdetermination in social theory. It is again necessary to turn to the definition provided by Brewster, who suggests overdetermination refers to:

the representation of dream thoughts in images privileged by their condensation of a number of thoughts in a single image (condensation), or by the transference of psychic energy from a particularly potent thought to apparently trivial things . . . [For Althusser] overdetermination of a contradiction is the reflection in it of its conditions of existence within the complex whole.

(in Althusser 1970)

Given that this is an attempt to develop means to think through Marx's theory, what is argued here is that the contradictions in the economic base of society can be regarded as determinant contradictions (comparable to Freud's potent thoughts) which overdetermine other more trivial instances by displacing on to them explosive energies.

But Baudrillard's conceptualization is different in important respects, for he uses the idea of overdetermination in a very un-Althusserian way, since he presents a discussion of *production processes as overdetermined by new forces of consumerism*, whereas the Althusserian conception would imply that Marxist theory would see a crisis like that of May '68 in France as 'overdetermined' by socio-economic class struggles, and this view was indeed elaborated by Althusser (in Macchiocchi 1973: 301–20). Baudrillard also, evidently, situates his thesis on the ground of the capitalist system of production in which production is the determinant moment. But here Baudrillard argues that the new structures of consumption are overdetermined by new ideologies and mythologies, corresponding to consumption as a productive force. The new process of over-determination signals the existence of a new phase in the evolution of capitalist society, of a significant internal displacement. The system is now overdetermined by ideological consumption, but it is production which still determines. In Althusserian terms, which could be used to reformulate this idea, this could be expressed perhaps to suggest that in the new phase of capitalist evolution, the capitalist mode of production has itself determined an internal shift from production to consumption now become the site of a dominant process. But the differences between the two formulations indicate not so much an epistemological divergence as one of substance and strategy.

It is worth exploring this difference in more detail. It seems clear that for Althusser's own project the idea of overdetermination is a concept which clarifies certain writings of Marx and Lenin where revolutionary crises are analysed as structural displacements, as entirely normal internal condensations of social contradictions. Baudrillard has made it clear that (for him) the evolution to a phase of capitalism in which consumption is a dominant moment is to be thought of as bringing society into a state (comparable to that) of 'generalized hysteria'. Elsewhere this idea is formulated in terms of the predominance of perverse desire. (The implication is that the current state is a *pathological* one.) It is possible to compare this idea with one Althusser developed in a critique of the current state of Marxism in the Soviet Union and beyond. Marxism itself was in a state of crisis, but one which had become 'blocked', giving rise to all the problems of 'deviations' within Marxist practices (see Althusser in Lecourt 1977); Althusser's conclusion was that the very undoing of the errors of practice is itself a political question.

Baudrillard's analysis of capitalist affluence remains very much at a diagnostic level: it is not that the crisis within consumerism is blocked, but that the very evolution into this condition is posed as a profound storing up of problems within the system in new and intensified forms, but in a way which withdraws the lever of action from the field of lived experience, from class relations.

Perhaps it might be argued that Baudrillard is drawing out some of the long-term implications of Marx's analysis of the negative internal resolution of capitalist contradictions. First, Baudrillard emphasizes the fact that the social form is a rapidly extended capitalism whose basic exchange mechanisms remain intact, resting on the increasing dominance of monopoly organization (with its fusions of finance and industrial capital). Second, there has been a corresponding evolution from the discipline of industrial labour in the nineteenth century to the modern process of the discipline of the consumer. Third, whereas in the early phases of capitalism it was the process of commodity production which dominated in conditions of the anarchic and anomic fields of consumption, now the field of consumption has become the principal one in which the object system has become codified: this resolution into capitalist affluence however has taken place as a negative resolution of the contradiction between human production and human needs; it has been 'resolved' in the denegation of pleasure. Fourth, the crucial use of the idea of overdetermination suggests that there are elements in the structure below those of the simple production–consumption cycle. It is all too easy to say, following Marx, that consumption reflects production. The way in which Baudrillard wants to examine this connection is not as a new form of class manipulation, or state apparatus, though this is certainly not ruled out. It is rather to follow through *the paradoxes of capitalist abundance in its hysterical symptomatology*. Thus, fifth, the strategy for the analysis of advanced capitalist formations tends to mirror not Althusser's analysis of capitalist forms but, paradoxically, Althusser's analysis of the symptomatology of the crisis in Marxism and the communist movement.[10] In this aspect what is crucial is the close linking of the idea of overdetermination to the specifically pathological signs of a system in crisis.

It seems that there are two quite different possible readings of Baudrillard's conception. It could be suggested that his analysis of capitalist consumerism as a development that exists in the mode of a general 'hysteria' can only imply that his analysis is simply normative. The tenor of his writing here would suggest that the predominant capitalist forms are distortions of a real, and genuine, human form of consumption. This would be a logical deduction given the fact that the model of hysteria is located by Freud as an abnormal form, against which a therapy can be evolved (based on the norm of what it is like not to be hysterical). As with all notions of 'alienation' or 'false consciousness' a truth is posited by the critique as its, often hidden, assumption and foundation.

But it would be unwise to jump to this conclusion, given the fact that Baudrillard has already indicated considerable critical distance from all theories of essential human needs or character, and thus from all essentialist theories of the satisfaction of needs. His criticism of Herbert Marcuse on this score is not only devastating but also marks out the terrain on which Baudrillard judges the validity of revolutionary strategies. Thus in Baudrillard's thought there is no appeal to human qualities which are alienated in a simple sense under modern capitalist processes, and no appeal is made to pre-requisite desires or needs of the individual or system. On the contrary, it is precisely the ideology of the sovereign consumer and the action of the individual pleasure-seeking consumer with all his need to enjoy the new abundance that is the dominant, 'overdetermining', mythology in modern society. It is the observation that all theories which begin with counterposing a need to the modern system of distribution are likely to be trapped within the system that indicates Baudrillard's determination to reach a transcendental analytical position.

Thus there is a second possible reading based on the view that the term overdetermination indicates the subtle preservation, not the elimination, of contradictions in the new phase of capitalist development. If consumption now becomes the site of a new immense social 'festival', 'spectacle', highly valorized in its cathectic 'realization' of the capitalist circulation process, its pleasure ideology 'overdetermines' the consumption process. In effect, if in the previous phase consumption was unregulated and its processes subject to the particular crisis of anomie, this was experienced often in the specific form of over- or under-production of goods relative to market demand and the recurrence of market booms and depressions. Now, says Baudrillard, the particular problem of the insatiability of demand has altered its form. It is no longer that proposed by Durkheim, where the deregulation or the breakdown of former norms gives rise to an explosion of insatiable 'needs', but rather the field becomes highly regulated by *new ideologically driven obligations which surge towards a new structure of insatiability that is not anomic*. The new structures do not attempt to bring into the light previously repressed or unsatisfied needs of an elemental kind. No appeal to 'essential' human requirements of this kind is made. Paradoxically, just at the moment when abundance is possible, says Baudrillard, a new phenomenon is created within capitalism, the strategic exploitation not of the producing but of the consuming masses. It is quite possible, he suggests, to view the new situation of the consumer as isolated, relatively powerless, subjected to the immense pressures of consumer advertising and the seductiveness of goods which have meaning only in the new ambient repressive structures of the new culture. This is experienced in the most contradictory of all possible ways: intense, repressive liberation, with its apparatuses of control, alienation, discipline, tending to produce within the system a new and powerfully *self-integrating class-differentiated social structure*. It is not therefore a question that the system creates 'false' needs in opposition to some more authentic ones which might exist at an individual level. The theory developed here suggests, rather, that late capitalism leads to a very specific form of the production of its own perverse needs, to be understood only on condition that the question of 'real' needs is put to one side.

We can easily see the significance of the approach that Baudrillard develops in *Consumer Society* by comparing it with that developed by Althusser at exactly the same time (1969–70), when the latter was elaborating a new theory of ideological state apparatuses. For the project which Althusser espoused at this time involved the formulation of 'an empirical list' of the major ideological apparatuses of the state (the religious, educational, familial, legal, political, trade union, and cultural apparatuses). In this discussion (Althusser 1971: 136) there was no place for consumerism at all. Instead of identifying consumerism as a decisive new ideological force for capitalist reproduction, Althusser gestured towards the functions of the family and the school as the crucial points of ideological reproduction. Since this period of writing other Althusserians, such as Balibar, have indicated considerable critical distance from these formulations in the direction of the specifically economic juridical ideologies themselves (Balibar 1985). In this respect Baudrillard remains in many senses on the ground of Marxist theory, giving more weight to economic and material processes in cultural analysis than other Marxists of this period. In a sense this also possibly protected him against the problematic teleological implications of regarding social reproduction from the vantage point of the state (for an assessment on this point see Gane 1983b). It is also highly paradoxical that Althusser's notion of interpellation was not more directly linked to a consideration of advertising, as already outlined by Barthes; ideologies of fashion, consumption for Althusser, unaccountably, were simply left to one side.

TOWARDS THE PACT WITH THE DEVIL

After these epistemological considerations let us now return to the analysis in *The Consumer Society*. The analysis identifies afresh the new ambience of social life, but now intensified in the account of the typical form: the modern shopping centre or airport, or the newly totally planned city shopping centre, as in the case of the Parisian suburban development Parly 2 (Baudrillard talks of Parlysians). Baudrillard's tone and analysis are ones of unconcealed contempt at this total homogenization, levelling of environment into a systematic attractive-repulse 'ambience', with its fountains and artificial vegetation evolved into a perpetual springtime. Here there is a commercial environment open seven days a week where virtually anything can be obtained by the new liquidity, via the credit card. Here is realized the total organization of everyday life, as a happy one. Nature itself appears, as does real life, sublimated into perpetual shopping. Matter has been processed as a new form of excretion just, ironically, at the moment money has dematerialized. Thus

> The substance of life, unified in this universal digest, can no longer have any meaning: that which produced dream work, the poetic work, the work of meaning, that is to say the grand schemas of displacement and condensation, the great figures of metaphor and contradiction, which are founded on the lived articulation of distinct elements no longer remains.
>
> (1988b: 35)

These observations develop a line of thought which becomes central to Baudrillard's later concerns, but here it is clear these remarks are deduced from a descriptive analysis. Yet this is quickly abandoned in this work.

What I have called Baudrillard's rapid transition from structural analysis to interpretation is nothing more, I think, than a transition to the second level of analysis which he has already identified as 'strategic', and what might at first sight be called Marxist (and I will remain with this at the moment, though I think it misses the dramatic meaning of this work). For what Baudrillard begins to analyse at this point is the fundamental misunderstanding which is sometimes reflected into Marxist theory itself of the true place of ideologies of equality and democratic equality in modern social life. These, he suggests, have always, even as processes of the formation of the modern subject, always been fragile in a society in which there were glaring forms of inequality of styles and levels of life. These ideologies and myths could really never carry the immense function theory gives them as integrative and legitimating mechanisms. It is much more likely that *the system counts on unconscious systems of integration, and this is precisely available in the sub-texts of consumer ideologies, which reproduce in a field of determinate and personalized differences a massive structure of implicit hierarchized and social relations* and which stand in marked contrast to formal doctrines of personal equality. In a capitalist society the gradual emergence of such ideologies of differentiation which overdetermine consumption practices is the equivalent of the resolution of a fundamental structural contradiction. And, for capitalism, the fact that this code exists at a specific level, absent as doctrine but present in its effects, means no revolution against it can be mobilized. Its effect therefore as a new regime of social discipline is overwhelmingly effective. It can be proposed, Baudrillard argues in functionalist vein, that this structure is admirably suited to replace in modern society all those social rituals which functioned as integrative, but hierarchized, mechanisms of primitive society, but hidden under the guise of self-interest.

At the end of the work Baudrillard returns to the themes of *The Object System*: consumer society is characterized as a society in which a new ambience emerges, but now this is also one of functional tolerance and a new sincerity (even the smile becomes part of the system). In the new society, ideologies which were once ferociously opposed are now in quiet 'dialogue'. But this tolerance is not wider than it once was; it has changed form into a new peaceful coexistence. But this is also true of forms of resistance. One of the paradoxes is that it combines violence and anti-violence, enthusiasm and despair. If the system cannot be transcended, this does not mean there is no resistance. But in this society there is violence, yet, without motive, it appears absurd or diabolic. The society of well-being, welfare, peace also has an obsession with security. Homeopathic doses of violence appear to act as vaccinations against fatality, in order to conjure away the real fragility of the system (1970: 278): another defeat for the revolution.

These forms, however, can be considered as indicating a more fundamental disequilibrium than is imagined, and can be grasped as anomie, and *anomalie*: from violence and delinquence to general fatigue, suicide, drugs, withdrawal. This cannot be envisaged from the interpretation of the consumer society as a liberation of all free subjects. But violence must be understood from the point of view of the new constraints, repressions. For, instead of allowing conflict to come to the surface, modern societies displace them into their code. On the surface all the discontents metamorphose into themselves in total functional tolerance (Hindu, Moslem, Buddhist, Hippies), a new ambience of tolerance and sincerity, a sentimental community, extremes join in the extremities in the moebius strip.[11] But the latent revolt can be seen in forms of fatigue and non-participation. In fact, excessive passivity can be regarded as more active than passive conformity. The revolt of May '68 was not an explosion, nor an inversion; it has to be conceived as conversion of one form of revolt into another. This society cannot release its inner tensions except by pathological displacement. Indeed, it is essential to analyse *consumption as a global process of 'conversion' in this sense, of transference in partial objects, and to generalize this theory to the process of 'somatization' on the basis of a theory of the body and its status as object in modernity.* The body is a kind of resumé of all the ambivalent processes: 'at the same time invested narcissistically as object of erotic solicitude, and invested "somatically" as object of anxiety and aggression' (1970: 296).

Baudrillard ends by considering the silent film, *The Student of Prague*, the story of a student who sells his reflected mirror image to the devil. This Other soon begins to intervene in the life of the student (it appears unexpectedly at a duel where it kills the adversary). It haunts him and makes his life impossible. Eventually the student tries to shoot and kill the double, only to find he has mortally wounded himself. Baudrillard comments: when our shadow escapes us, it falls into the hands of the devil. It can escape us, we cannot escape it. 'The object (soul, shadow, the product of our labour become object) takes revenge' (1970: 395). In the logic of alienation, there is no alternative but death. It is the structure of the pact with the devil.[12]

Chapter 6

From production to reproduction

Capital abolishes social determination through the mode of production

Baudrillard

A REORGANIZATION OF PROBLEMS

Baudrillard's book *Symbolic Exchange and Death* was published in 1976, six years after *Consumer Society*. It is an attempt to develop a general examination of the differences between the symbolic and the semiological order. It is no doubt a brilliant and subtle work, written as theory (it provides very little in the way of empirical analysis or example in its 340 pages), yet it is clear that it is not written from the point of view of orthodox Marxism or that of modern social science in any simple sense. On the contrary, it appears to entail a critique of modern social science from the point of view of 'primitive', utopian, symbolic exchange. It involves, in a sense, Baudrillard's attempt to stand back from the analysis of consumer society and consider the position from which from now on his critique of it will be made.

It is clear from previous discussion that Baudrillard had begun to talk in earnest of taking up a position 'outside' commodity exchange itself. In a sense this can be seen to relate to a question which has arisen many times in the Marxist tradition. Perhaps the most famous discussion can be found in Lenin's notion that, as workers located within the production process itself, proletarians can achieve only a level of trade union consciousness, and this can never by itself achieve a breakthrough to a level of strategic political transcendence. Only on the basis of a perspective of a more extensive kind can a genuine political position develop that is adequate to a struggle of a revolutionary type. In Lenin's own theoretical analysis of Russian society, he identified not one but many modes of production themselves articulated in an order of domination. The socialist, co-operative, and communal forms were to be the basis of a struggle of displacement of the dominant capitalist forms. But nevertheless the aim was hardly in doubt in Lenin's conception: the struggle for a communist society based on a communist mode of production.

Baudrillard's position, by the mid-1970s, rejected the idea that the critique of capitalism should be based on the notion of an alternative mode of production, even a communist one. From this point onwards Baudrillard attempted to elaborate a quite new version of this alternative which could perhaps be thought of as cultural communism, except that its contours and its content are quite remote from anything envisaged by Marx.[1] The ideas developed by Durkheim and Mauss on the other hand, as the writing of Bataille revealed, lead to an alternative version of primitive culture and to a conception of socialism from which it is possible to derive a powerful critique of Marxism.

Although Baudrillard was significantly influenced by Mauss's conception of the gift and counter-gift, the influence of Bataille's attempt to connect the gift to a larger framework which breaks profoundly with any productivism is more in evidence.[2] What concerns Baudrillard is not so much an attempt to compare modern society with its own ideal, as can be seen to appeal to Durkheim and Mauss in their conception of pathological forms, but rather to develop an abstract principle from which it is possible to develop a new critique of modern society. For Durkheim and Mauss modern society was not in need of transcendence but of treatment, of cure. For Baudrillard, the problem is one that is much closer to that of Marx: the struggle for a basis of a revolutionary critique, but now without a revolutionary subject.[3]

Symbolic Exchange and Death (1976) marks a stage of considerable deepening of Baudrillard's fundamental theory, and it works towards a new programme of work which, although being in a sense more concentrated than that of 1972 (see Gane 1991: 84), is perhaps more powerful, and relates to the question: is there a higher and more subversive logical form than the present system of simulations? But before that question is reached Baudrillard in some senses recapitulates his own development in the first sections of the book before developing new aspects of his conception of symbolic exchange in studies of death and of the poetic. This generally appears as a step back in order to relaunch an attack of contemporary cultural and political structures. Though, in effect, the objective is to determine the answer to a more intractable question: *how does the culture of the sign, of production, succeed in its reduction of the symbolic order?*

The work begins therefore with another essay on the importance of production, as if the ghost had not yet been satisfactorily exorcized.[4] But it underlines and makes his change of position from classical Marxism irreversible. In this discussion several important implications are clarified, as Baudrillard discusses strikes and the situation of the proletariat in post-May '68 France. The book begins with a ringing declaration of his new position, that the radical implications of Mauss's study of the gift and Saussure's study of anagrams will

appear in the long term, as more radical hypotheses than those of Freud and Marx.

(1988b: 119)

Marx and Freud are certainly not abandoned, but have to be approached in a critical fashion so that the radical elements are made available to analysis. All structuralist appropriations of these writers have to be questioned at a fundamental level since they all tend to draw interpretation towards productivist assumptions and principles.

The radical interpretation of capitalism and its culture leads towards the recognition of the importance of the gift and the counter-gift, the reversibility of life and death, of the reversibility of the terms of an anagram, not in any attempt to reduce the question to a mystique, or a new structuralism, but towards a new 'ineluctable' form (for the Durkheim roots of the term reversibility see Caillois 1959). Fundamentally, in order to understand this, Baudrillard argues, it is necessary to analyse the way in which the modern idea of reality, the reality principle, was connected to a phase of the evolution of western society, a phase which was reflected in the theory of political economy (itself, resting on the law of value in use and exchange). Today the system is increasingly indeterminate; reality has been displaced, in the consumer society, by the 'hyper-reality' of the code. For this system has abolished the effectivity of 'external reality' (which was brought into existence with the first order of simulation), and with it the play of ideologies which it structured in depth. It is possible to construct a genealogy, one step on from that in *Consumer Society*, which will reveal the place of political economy and production in the long term process. Once there was a capitalist mode of production: but now a new form has emerged in which capital itself has lost its former characteristics. And as each stage succeeds a former one, the earlier one is taken as a phantom model of 'reality' for the later. These are not simple transitions:

> these are the true revolutions . . . it is only in the third order that theory and practice, themselves fl\ .ting and indeterminate, can catch up with the hyperreal and strike it dead.
>
> (1988b: 121)

This idea has to be understood in terms of Baudrillard's conception of the evolution of simulacra, now conceived in relation to objects, not class fractions and cultural strategies.[5] Historical consciousness, he argues in this reorganized problematic, itself corresponds to the age of the machine; the modern unconscious corresponds, however, to a world become indeterminate. The unconscious itself has become part of the whole system and all elements have become subject to manipulation. *The new order that arises is one of an ungraspable system of simulations.* The reality and certainty of the dialectic has gone, to be replaced by genetic codes and random combinations. Even critical theory and political revolution become things of the past, and belong to the old order,

> no longer the basis of modern simulation. It is useless to try to resurrect the dialectic, 'objective' contradictions . . . that is a political regression without hope.
>
> (1988b: 122, trs. mod.)

Against the new order a strategy of dialectical transcendence is of no avail. The system has effectively neutralized all first order (natural systems) and second order (dialectic) strategies; it has passed to a higher level, one which has become 'definalized', which can therefore absorb and counter all oppositions based on finalities. It is necessary, he argues, to find a form of dissent which is at an even higher level of logical strategy than the system itself; all others fail. Thus the major objective for any new programme of work must be the search for such a strategic formulation.

But much rests on Baudrillard's conception of the state of the present system and his analysis at this point is surprising. In spite of all appearances, the present system is fragile, it will take only a 'straw' (*coup de pouce*) to make the whole system tumble.[6] No long process of dialectical struggle is necessary, since the whole weight of the increased inertia of the system begins to set in motion a terminal phase. At the point of complete functionality and 'ideal coherence' the system becomes vulnerable, sick. As it comes close to 'radical indetermination' it is unable to deal with the re-emergence of meaning and begins to collapse under its own density.

In these conditions a new strategy must avoid reduplicating past assumptions. It must pass from the transcendental to the cata-strophic. This is not to be based on an internal logical structure of opposition or contradiction, but rather on a logic of the system: continued beyond its own limits the system will turn in on itself. It will naturally invert, through the intensification of its inherent ambivalence. He sums up this perspective:

> the only strategy of opposition to a hyperrealist system is pata-physical, a 'science of imaginary solutions': in other words, a science fiction about the system returning to destroy itself, at the extreme limit of simulation, a reversible simulation in a hyper-logic of destruction and death.
>
> (1988b: 123)

The structural violence of the code meets its equivalent at this point where value is abolished.

Baudrillard reflects that his conception of the political economy of the sign (1972) was essentially a compromise position, which has to be reformulated in the new conditions. In the new context, of the third order of simulation (coexistent with monopoly finance capital), capital itself begins to abolish labour and production and indeed political economy as well. The dialectic of signifier and signified is pushed to the limit as is the notion of use and exchange. The code reaches a stage of maximal intensification:

> it is not the revolution which puts an end to all this, but capital itself. Capital abolishes social determination through the mode of production, and substitutes the structural form of value for the commodity form. And it is capital that determines the current strategy of the system.
>
> (1988b: 128, trs. mod.)

The code (of capital) reduces everything in the end to undecid-ability, a 'generalized brothel' of interchangeability, and this has already begun to affect the so-called infrastructure (the economic).

It is no longer possible to regard it, even theoretically, as a determining structure.

Political economy must change therefore before the new structural law of value as the very basis of the social begins to disappear (in this new phase of capitalism without a mode of production). Ironically, Baudrillard here follows the letter of Althusser's own formulation of moving in principle from the primacy of production to that of reproduction. But Baudrillard's intentions are directed to quite different forms of analysis: not to the radicalization of the revolutionary principle of class struggle (now deemed a thing of a past era), but to the idea that the primacy of reproduction destroys all possibility and all hope of revolution in the form of active sacrifical class struggle. Now, under the new regime of the structural law of value, work is no longer primarily productive. It, too, has become reproductive. The Althusserian terms have been turned back against themselves in a strange new sociology of theoretical Marxism (the principle of which was enunciated by Lefebvre).[7] The culture loses its fascination with productivity as a fundamental creative function, and work becomes valued in its own right as simply work. Work in fact becomes a simulation of its former self, and is, in the process, dramatically emptied of all real content. It is a form which now has to reproduce itself for its own sake.

IRONY OF MARXISM

In light of this idea and this outcome, Marx was perhaps more in error about labour and production than the Luddites, Baudrillard argues, for they foresaw the possibility of a truly catastrophic end of capitalism.[8] Marx, on the other hand, was led to analyse the process as a long dialectical struggle, with a triumphant overturning of capitalism as its outcome. In retrospect this was, he suggests, perhaps only a 'dream' developed in the wake of the defeats of the early phase of struggles and the realization of the impossibility of revolution. The new period today marks the end of this dream, and perhaps the (re)emergence of other possibilities. But from now on, notes Baudrillard, there is no point in trying to rescue Marxism on this point: the transcendental social dialectic is dead.

The problem today is to begin to analyse the new nature of this work. This is best done by following its own disengagement with its purposes, a perspective that can also make work appear as something distinct from any particular job or position, on the pattern of an ambience. *Work itself today has become something abstract and interchangeable*. It has become a code which seeks to fix the particular positions in 'work'; it is an abstract 'operator' which extends across the whole institutional sphere, even if the concrete meaning of work has passed irretrievably into history. With this increasing abstraction come ideas of job enrichment, deepening the quality of working life, even job 'personalization' and job sharing: everyone is to be embraced in a new and total framework of participation and manipulation. The previous system with its direct buying and selling of labour has been transformed, *now the conception of consumption predominates even in the sphere of production*. Previously, as in Marx, consumption had to be understood as having its place determined by production. Now it is

the opposite. We must conceive of the entire sphere of production, of work and the productive forces, as afloat in the sphere of 'consumption' understood as a generalised axiomatic of the coded exchange of signs.

(1989b: 10)

In this new phase, then, the old equivalences disappear: the wage is no longer related to the performance of a specific kind of labour, except as the reproduction of previous expenditure. Now the performance of labour, as work, is more like a simple ritual, a 'baptism' which turns the individual into a citizen. This is the meaning behind all the massive efforts made in recent years so that unemployment can be avoided. Work is invested in the worker not the other way round. When this happens on a wide scale and the sign function of work becomes predominant, the old idea of a fair wage also begins to disappear and new, quite unlimited demands begin to come forward. In fact, he suggests, this can be read as a new and dramatic appearance of a new challenge to the basic code: maximum wage for minimum work (1989b: 16). It indicates that workers have become non-workers: their strategy has become a catastrophic one. It is perhaps part of a process in which purely productive work has become obsolescent in the system. An irony arises: from workers in opposition to exploitation, the new condition suggests maximal compensation for workers for loss of exploitation.

In this light the strike changes its character. Once it was justified on the grounds that it confronted the violence of capitalist oppression and exploitation. This notion and type of strike is at an end. Capital will simply allow a company to perish in order for capitalism to continue as a system; or the strike will be seen to yield only what the system would have otherwise yielded on its own. Sometimes a simple class struggle erupts, but this is usually where immigrant labour is involved and because unions have not been able to swallow it into the system. This creates so many problems for unions that within a short time, even these immigrant workers are absorbed, often to the call to class struggle.

In one of his few appeals to an empirical case Baudrillard at this point presents a discussion of the Renault strike in 1973, which he claims was sparked off by immigrant workers in a wild-cat action. The CGT initially spread the strike, but lost control when workers spontaneously returned to work. The unions were caught in the middle of the action. Their overtures rejected on all sides. In terms of the social system this spells danger, a loss of control in a vital sector, as the unions have become an institutional bulwark: the unions saved the regime as a whole in 1968 (1989b: 21).[9] The very notion of the strike today has become indeterminate –

the workers go back to work with no gain having refused an offer with sensible gains eight days before. . . . In fact this confusion is dream like; it translates a capital fact, one that is difficult for the proletarians themselves to accept: that the social struggle has displaced the traditional external class enemy, capital and the bosses, onto the true internal class enemy, their own representative authority of class: the party or union.

(1989b: 21)

The effect of this displacement whereby 'parties and unions alienate the social power of the exploited (and) monopolise its representation' leads to uncertainty and apparent regression. In fact, however, it reveals that conventional parties and unions are a thing of the past. It only remains for them to pass away (1989b: 22).

An important conclusion can be drawn from this, he argues. The analysis of May '68 and the subsequent strikes reveals a profound crisis in systems of representation, and a profound moral corruption of the proletariat under modern capitalism. It is the immigrant worker who reveals the new situation in all its complexity, and the relationship of workers to their own labour power . . . and this is because they are the ones who have most recently been uprooted from a non-productivist tradition.

(1989b: 22)

The effect of the introduction of non-European labour, then, was to bring increasing unrest and discontent, and this brought about a new phenomenon:

this time . . . the workers stopped work, just like that, suddenly, not claiming anything and negotiating nothing, to the great despair of the unions and the bosses, and then they started work spontaneously and together the following Monday . . . a 'work-stop'. A euphemism that says much more than the term 'strike': the whole discipline of work tumbles, all the moral norms and practices that have been imposed in the two centuries of industrial colonisation in Europe are shattered and forgotten, without any apparent effort, without any 'class struggle' to speak of . . . just do what is necessary and come back later.

(1989b: 22)

Immigrant workers have been reproached, especially by colonialists, for their attitudes and behaviour: their laxity, their erratic attendance, indifference to wages and incentives, to overtime, to promotion, in short, their irrational culture. This gives witness, says Baudrillard, to vast cultural difference. The introduction of non-European workers to countries like France has meant a difficult process of training them to a new work ethic, but, ironically, this happened just at the very moment when European workers began to adopt practices which corrupted old norms. The new attitudes to employment are cool and cynical and far from traditional modes of confrontation. The work ethic is now a fragile remainder: more of a collective paranoia which became a morality and then a myth, but which is now disintegrating.

In these completely new circumstances an increasing number of strikes occur without any apparent economic or political meaning; but they are significant as they are, in an important sense, says Baudrillard trying to develop this new line of argument, gestures against production for its own sake. This is consistent with the profound displacement in the economy – the strike for the sake of the strike is simply a logical continuation of its 'inverse tautology'. Yet even in this form it is dangerously subversive, because, as it displaces the finalities of the previous order, it becomes a radical parody of them: one which 'denies on its own ground the endless finality' of production. Sociological and economic critiques of the system, which previously identified the problem of its wasteful nature, were all rather pious. Today the characteristic which has become prominent is not waste but rather, he notes (no doubt falling into a position which is the exact reverse of complete functionalism), objective uselessness, complemented however by the demand from all sides that the system reproduce employment for everyone. Employment has become the equivalent of a socially distributed product: as productive labour is reduced by technical progression, so the capitalist system has to provide more work. More and more the demand is pressed that strike time be paid for, so that the new strike form can be guaranteed.

When the dramatic transition occurs, and production is dominated by reproduction, production is no longer dominated by production for use or for exchange. The paradox must be grasped in full irony, he insists. The worker reproduces his own 'work'. And all consumption has become reproductive consumption (leisure is indistinguishable from work), and all economic sectors, like the service sector, become as 'productive' as industry. In this new order capitalism is not dominated by the money form, or by reification, but is a pure social relation: production must be seen (as it always was, in fact, but now above all) as a modality of reproduction of the code. Previously this productive modality was predominant, but now reproduction is the dominant mode of reproduction itself. If this is posed in terms close to those of Michel Foucault (whose work on genealogies had a profound effect on Baudrillard, who takes the idea and forces it beyond the fields of application in Foucault), it is as if the factory form has disappeared only to blossom as an infinite expansion. As the seventeenth-century system of confinement set industrial work on its way towards the factory, it did so by imposing a new rationalized ordering of disciplined work on its deviants. Against the visions of a liberation from work as such (a dominant utopian vision to the mid-1970s) this discipline is generalized into a society that has become a vast detention camp of labour-for-the-sake-of-labour. If this is truly the case, then the whole theory of social stratification has to be rewritten. For it is now clear that Marx's theory of the proletariat as principally defined through its exploitation and its oppression has to be replaced by a theory of stratification on the basis, not of exploitation, but of *excommunication* (a concept which makes its dramatic return in Baudrillard's work *America*).

It is thus clear that the tendency of Baudrillard's thought is strangely consistent in its rapprochement with Durkheim's theory of outsider groups (see Gane 1983b). Baudrillard expresses this in a typically forthright way: there has never been a true class struggle except on the basis of such discrimination, on the basis of sub-humans against their status, in the case of the proletariat against a caste status which consigns it to subhumanity of labour. Thus, as soon as the western working classes are accepted into society as normal human subjects, they begin to adopt all the usual discriminatory practices of the normal against the abnormal: they become racist, sexist, ageist. The proletariat adheres to a culture which opposes and represses the deviant, the mad, the outsider. There is no difference here between the bourgeois and the proletarian, and it reveals the crucial fact that the basic law of modern society is not that of exploitation, it is, as Foucault argued, that of normalization.

One of the crucial and revelatory effects of the displacement of production towards reproduction was established in May '68. This is clearly visible in the fact that it was the university faculties of social and human sciences that were the points of explosion: it was these faculties which felt the first intimations of the new order of total uselessness and the new predominance of reproductive labour. The explosion cannot be seen as a blockage in the system of productive labour which acted as the closure of a pressure valve in the system, except in the sense that real productive work was no longer available, for the system as a whole cannot offer genuine 'work' any more. The first intimations of the new order were registered in the 'superstructure', in the sphere of university culture which recognized the end of an historical epoch. This recognition soon spread throughout society, and all social struggles are influenced by it. At first the young, the marginal, those at the edges of the system registered it in the strongest terms. The last groups to become aware of these changes are the traditional working-class groups who have been trained on all sides to think of labour as productive, even the source of all social wealth (Marx).

This whole complex of labour mythology is now revealed in its own right in all its ramifications. It can be seen that the illusion of production is fully integrated into a specific vision of freedom on the one hand and leisure on the other. The very significance given

to productive labour itself had functioned to mitigate exploitation
and to give it meaning. The production of use values is really only
an ideological formation which transposes itself into a moral ideal.
But those groups who have been most fully saturated in this illusion
are those least capable of responding to the new situation and its
new opportunities. They are revealed as the most highly integrated
and mystified of all social groups, and all movements which reflect
this in (Marxist) social theory must be included in this category. A
provocation tc the left: only when these groups become conscious
of the place of labour in the new system of the reproduction of useless work will an explosion such as that of May '68 be generalized
throughout society.

Baudrillard, then, turns the Althusserian notion of reproduction
into an irony of orthodox Marxism. There are some points in common: first, both see the proletariat as having the final deciding
voice and the role of the French Communist Party as having been
less than revolutionary. And both see the crucial problems as lying
in the sphere of reproduction (of the conditions of production). But
Althusser and the Althusserians argued that this must still be seen
as a form of class struggle determined in the last instance by
economic processes in the capitalist mode of production which produces surplus value on which the parasitic groups reproduce themselves. In this context the structure and function of the state loom
large, and its analysis becomes increasingly important. But for
Baudrillard, this form of thinking (though it might be possible for
his theses to be reformulated in terms of the state) is contained in a
framework now inverted. For Baudrillard, May '68

> only translated the chasm in the current system between those
> who still believed in their own labour-power, and those who did
> not.
>
> (1989b: 26)

THE ANNIHILATION OR IRONY OF SYMBOLIC EXCHANGE?

This discussion of reproduction is seen as a specific case of the displacement of political economy by the structural law of value as a
simulation model. This theme is developed vigorously, not as a
simple argument that the 'economic' as such has disappeared from
view, but rather that the cash nexus now appears directly in view as

an obscenity. This is discussed in relation to recent bank advertising. This states blatently: your money interests me – give and take – let me take your money and I will make you profit from my bank (Baudrillard 1976: 53–4).[10] Now, at first sight of course this looks like a direct appeal to the reciprocity of exchange. But Baudrillard is not concerned with this. His analysis suggests that what is in evidence here is a departure from all previous restraint in advertising in the knowledge that there was a certain age-old immorality in profiting from interest. Certainly this new level of advertising marks a distinct break in the degree of directness: a kind of advertising based on an approach that is essentially man-to-man, he argues, a 'virile complicity' – it is time to lay out the cards on the table and to face the triumphant obscenity of capitalist functioning as if it were all out in the open. Everyone can fix their eyes on money as if it were a sexual object. The technique, he notes taking the point to an obscenity himself, is one of 'perverse provocation', as if the bank were saying, in Baudrillard's words, your arse interests me, give me your buttocks and I will bugger you and you will enjoy it (1976: 54). It is quite different in intensity from the advertisement of a competing bank which simply expresses the view that it is the customer who should have the smile not the banker, now seen to be a ploy belonging to a previous era of advertising, but of course Baudrillard is interested not in any constraining effect this may have, only in the logic of the obscenity itself.

Thus capital does not abide by the old rules any longer. The old law of value can now be manipulated at will. And this can be done on a number of different levels: your unconscious interests me, for example, could now be expressed by psychoanalysts. And in so far as this spreads right across social fields it leads to a process whereby all social relations become inflected by this new obscenity. In advertising this is realized in a new realism: a bank is a bank. A state of affairs is presented as a facticity, as an untranscendable institutional arrangement, a tautology, and a fundamental rule of domination. Against this new form an appeal to revolutionary forces is lost since all energies return to the system and are easily absorbed. This is because the basic structures are quite different from any symbolic exchange or dialectical progression. The new order is one of simulation in the third degree, typically of obscenity, of naked and brutal provocation which cannot be countered on its own terms, since there is no longer any internal play of oppositional force within the system (defined by Baudrillard in a way, unfortunately, that makes this a tautology – or perhaps that which does not conform to the code simply disappears from his view).

The only hope of action against this system lies outside it, he repeats, in the symbolic violence of which the gift and counter-gift are the paradigm. But this idea has now to be deepened and understood in its full alterity (1976: 63), a term which will become important in Baudrillard's later work, as radical alterity (1990b). It is not a new mysticism of the gift and of altruistic motives based on individualistic assumptions. It is not in any sense a question of gratuitous acts of individuals. Baudrillard does not stress the conventional force of obligation (Mauss), but he suggests that the primitives know that the gift is a challenge, and it is annulled only in the counter-gift. This characteristic of the gift as reversible has to be recognized as different from any mode of contractual exchange. In primitive cultures the ambivalence of death in exchange is fully acknowledged. In our culture the two poles of the exchange are broken, and each side breaks off into a remote autonomy.

It is in this perspective that hostage taking can be seen not only as a simple process of establishing the demand for ransom, etc., but also as establishing the irruption of the symbolic order itself against the system, and at bottom this is the only possible revolution against it. In terms of a terrorist challenge to the system the only possible answer seems to be the death of the terrorist, but this leaves the challenge completely unanswered. In return for a challenge in the form of an escalation to the level of symbolic challenge of death to the system only a counter-death is appropriate. The immense system of powers in the west seems unable to respond to this kind of challenge since beyond the specific act itself is another cultural order which, in its particular way, calls for a specific sacrifice, one which cannot be acceded. This was also the case in May '68, for the basic demand of the students was posed at the level of symbolic exchange: this kind of challenge is incapable of being absorbed. The martyr, when created, always poses a fundamental ambivalence. It is the same in the Christian tradition, for the veiled aim of self-sacrifice to God is to reach towards a position in which God cannot contain the debt. At that point the relative positions of the sacrificer and God are reversed.[11] This explains why these activities always approach heresy and always have to be rigorously controlled by the religious authorities. Such exchanges are controlled by the church in a way which prevents them becoming catastrophic. It is done by establishing a hierarchical order of exchanges but always in order to lead to an equivalence between the sacrificer and God. This implies that a gift which is irreversible is a threat to the order itself. Institutions in general have therefore to control exchanges and to ensure that a catastrophic situation is avoided. In this respect the challenge of hostage taking is fascinating for the modern order since it mirrors the exorbitant violence of the social system at the same time as it threatens it with death.

It is now possible to return to reproduction, since some of the patterns of exchange are clarified if the relation between capital and labour is looked at in this, extremely unusual, even perverse, version of exchange theory, taken, in a way that defines Baudrillard's distinctiveness as a theorist, to the limit: death. In a sense the violence of physical exploitation of the worker pales into insignificance in comparison with the violence perpetrated against the symbolic order of the worker, for the main stake is always symbolic. All exchange between capital and labour presupposes the 'extermination' of objects, and it is only death, not labour power or abstract labour, that enables an equivalence to be established. In this case the workers' death is not an immediate and sudden dangerous sacrifice: it is slow and prolonged. The opposite of this kind of work is not leisure or free time. Its opposite is the total and immediate sacrifice. The liberation of the slave or serf has made possible the free worker; he is the slave 'liberated' for work. And it is here, he argues wickedly, that capital installs death. In this particular capitalist form, the worker is put to a differed death and this is the specific power of capital. For the slow controlled death of the worker changes nothing – it is not a challenge. Revolution puts death back into play in the system into its own time, which is the rhythm of symbolic exchange itself, for symbolic exchanges are rendered in their own specific cycle.[12] The strategy of capital is clearly that of interrupting and breaking this cycle and to subordinate it to a linear time. In this time the worker is rendered to capital in infinitesimal portions.

This, then, is an immediate hypothesis which can be drawn from a critique of the traditionally established capitalist system from the point of view of symbolic orders: the worker submits his life to the exploiter and this is successful to the extent that the latent power of the return is displaced in time, and therefore cannot cancel the sphere of power. It is then displaced from the sphere of any resolution. In fact, it now appears that the worker donates capital to the employer and in return the capitalist provides work to the worker:

it is in the power of the capitalist to initiate the gift. The refusal of work is therefore radical; it is the refusal of symbolic domination. The poisoned character of this exchange is the mark of the wage, the dominant social code.[13] The strategic aim of capital is to limit the exchange to a contract and to stabilize, control and manipulate this relation. The refusal of work always reveals that what is at stake is an exchange of an order which is more fundamental in its totality and implication, and it puts the initial gift into question.

But this traditional set of relations is no longer in place. Today, the wage is given in order that it is spent (and this itself is considered a kind of work), which is the entry of another kind of slow death as a regime into the system. Now the object enters the system not as something that can be offered up as a sacrifice in exchange: it becomes an object that is used and consumed to death in use. This is altogether different from the way that a gift is consumed as a pure loss. It is now possible to see that in the past the exercise of power was open and direct in the festival in the sacrifice. And reversion was always a possibility. After the decline of master–slave dialectic the major formation became one of the reproduction of power itself. And today, even the buying back of power has to be simulated, it cannot be accomplished openly and directly on the ground of the system itself. *In this sense the truly unprecedented nature of capitalism is revealed as a completely new solution to the problem of power.*[14] The increasing scale of modern economic forms has brought a new form of control over symbolic exchanges through production at first, but now it occurs through consumption. The economic succeeds again in masking its structure.

This striking analysis is then generalized apparently in the most facile manner, and an equally facile manner can also be found in his analysis of the media. Here there is a monopoly of control such that what is produced is always a message without a response. Or, to take the transport system: what is produced is a gift in the form of a network of roads. Yet the return, the vast number of deaths (the accident has its place in this order), is a hopelessly inadequate attempt to counter social power. Nevertheless however hopeless, these counter-gifts cannot find an adequate response from the system. If the system tries to absorb them the problem is only made worse; they are incompatible. Thus the theory of the gift is the basis of a unification of understanding across many fields, from May '68, terrorism, to work and consumption. It is based on the view that contrary to all humanist, or libertarian, or Christian ideology, the gift is the source and essence of power. Only the counter-gift can abolish it.

(1976: 73)

Marcel Mauss would have been astonished to have seen what consequences could be derived from his essay by a theorist engaged in unrestrained (by the real, by moral structures, by fear of consequences) analysis from the point of view of the gift as an absolute principle, in the spirit of *détournement*.

Chapter 7

Modernity, simulation, and the hyperreal

*the entire system of communication has passed from that of a
syntactically complex language structure to binary sign system*
Baudrillard

MODERNITY'S COMPLEXITY

Baudrillard's approach to contemporary culture is certainly dominated by the theme of modernization, and a consideration of his short
article on modernity (1987f) must form an essential part of any
genuine assessment of Baudrillard's approach to contemporary
cultural analysis. Written in the early 1970s at a moment when
Baudrillard's thought was still heavily influenced by Bachelardian–
Althusserian epistemological notions, his essay specifically notes
that there can be no genuine theory of modernity, it is not a theoretical object only a particular logic and an accompanying ideology.
Hence there are in fact only 'traits' of modernity which, at one level,
tend to a particular homogeneity in great contrast to the immense
diversity of traditional cultures. Yet modernity implies change, and
constant changefulness, in contrast to the stability of other cultures.

The term, he suggests, has a strong meaning only in societies
where there are long cultural traditions (it has little meaning in the
USA). But in Europe, since the Renaissance, it is in the catholic
countries that modernity has had most significance, since the
church itself has constantly tried to keep abreast of new cultural
currents, to modernize (for example the Jesuits). In European
history, modernism has been associated with the rise of individualist philosophical rationalism, science, and technology. In the early
phase there was continual opposition between ancient and modern
forms, but it was only in the nineteenth century that 'modernity'

itself became an identifiable phenomenon (with Gautier and Baudelaire). The logic of modernity is that of linear temporal progression, reflected in the idea of history as a teleological and irreversible accumulation. In culture, culminating in the last two centuries, modernity results in an aesthetic of individual creativity, of the avant-garde, and of fashion. This complements linear time with a specific form of the fashion cycle in which all past cultural forms are recreated, abstracted out of previous contexts, and enter into a completely new order of sign exchanges. When this becomes dominant, modernity itself ceases to be a transcendent system, there is no longer the possibility of internal revolutions: 'it nourishes itself on the vestiges of all cultures in the same way that it does from technical gadgets or from the ambiguity of all values' (1987f: 69). Therefore it can be said that modernity is not to be thought of as a revolution against, but as arising specifically in a certain 'subtle cultural play' with, traditional forms. This is more clearly visible in the impact of western on Third World cultures. Analysis 'based on a dialectic of rupture must give way to an approach which recognizes the dynamic of amalgamation . . . modernity is paradoxical rather than dialectical' (1987f: 70).

It is therefore not very easy or straightforward, he suggests, to evaluate modernity. Political and social changes are important, but these never constitute its basic features. Once modernity has become dominant, its forms, in fact, restrict and block structural social change. In everyday life, modernity as culture becomes dominated by the mass media and by modern gadgetry. In this sense, it is clear that modernity is an effect of combined technological and cultural processes. It is certainly an error to see in modernity a process of rationalization, or one in which the individual as such becomes sovereign.[1] Indeed, the reactionary celebration of individual subjectivity occurs at the same time as a massive homogenization of culture, that is when subjectivity is recycled in new forms of 'personalisation'. Modernity is more and more taken up with 'the formal play of change' for its own sake. Paradoxically its own myths of progress and technical control eventually return to haunt modern societies as this mastery is realized to be itself the myth of modernity. In modern societies:

liberty is formal, people become masses, culture becomes fashion. Once a dynamic of progress, modernity is slowly becoming an activism of well being.

(1987f: 72)

It is important to note that Baudrillard's later writing on America does not develop in terms of an analysis of post-modernity, but of modernity, and even 'radical modernity' and 'eccentric modernity' (1988a: 81). The cultural structure of modernity is investigated by a new theory (and a new way of theorizing) of the stages of its internal evolution, which he calls a genealogy of simulation.

This is the most problematic of all of Baudrillard's writing, and is the site of some subtle and some very unsubtle thinking. It is necessary to be ready to intervene, if this has not already been done, in order not to be carried away with the rapid escalation of stakes. On the whole, it is clear that there have been some very serious changes made to his project which amount to a complete abandonment of academic, scientific styles of work: his work in fact proceeds as if he believed that the reality principle had disintegrated, and no longer applied in the social realm. This is certainly shocking to read, but it is not of the slightest relevance to say, at this juncture, the real world still exists. His experiment is posed in such a way that the real has been withdrawn, and, as a consequence he is forced into fiction-theory. But the gains come in the theory of simulation and eventually in the new analysis of complex objects, which could not have been done if this period had not been fertile.

SIMULATION

Baudrillard elaborates the genealogy of the orders of simulation over the period of European history since the Renaissance.[2] This is, no doubt, only a sketch, yet it rivals that of Foucault *The Order of Things* (1970), in its vast ambitions to elaborate not theoretical modes production but modes of simulation. In a sense Baudrillard's purpose is to provide a background to the modern order of simulation, the hyperreal, posed against the framework of the division between the orders of symbolic exchange itself, followed by semiological orders now reconceptualized as simulation.

A. Symbolic exchange
  i) characteristic reversibility of primitive cultures
  ii) hierarchized systems with restricted movement of signs: power through control over exchanges
B. Simulation (phases of cultures of accumulation)
  i) renaissance–classical period: nature/counterfeited nature

ii) the industrial period: natural/the produced counterpart
   (both periods i and ii are premissed on the 'real')
iii) post-industrial period: produced/simulated hyperreal model.

Baudrillard's aim here is to show that no adequate analysis of
systems of representation can, simply, refer to the 'real' world (the
referent), as if this was unproblematic. Indeed, it is necessary to
include in any discussion the emergence of the very conception of
the real world, and 'nature', in its proper context. What tends to
happen, he argues, is that in each phase of representation a former,
dominant conception of the 'real' is taken as the reference model of
'current' reality, always already out of date. For example, in discourse today it is possible to find reference to a nature that is above
any social practice: this is comprehensible only as a reference to
assumptions produced in a previous period, which still have a
current effectivity. Thus the historical sequence, as genealogy, has
the characteristic of being a classification, but also one that is
dynamic and folded back on itself.

   Baudrillard takes as his example of classical notions of simulation, the stucco imitation of velvet curtains and wooden objects,
the stucco imitation of flesh. The riot of stucco imitation in the
rococo period seems to exemplify the arrival of a new substance
used as a basis of reducing to a new level of equivalences all previous diversities. In this he finds a theoretical parallel with the
project of the Jesuits, who perhaps discovered key modern features
of modern power, since they attempted to reunify the world on the
basis of an homogeneous doctrine and to create a world in its like-
ness: a new political élite, a new administrative apparatus, a new
educational system, all of which could be interchanged, because
they formed a homogeneous system of values. All things here take
on an aspect of functionality (note, he suggests, even their doctrine
of the functionality of the cadaver (1976: 88)). Such perverse
coherence prefigures that of the commodity exchange system as a
homogenizing system. It culminates in a closed world based on a
universal substance, rather like the world of the artist who models
everything in concrete or plastic.

   The culture of the classical world was of course more complex
than the Jesuit one. Baudrillard discusses its theatrical model of the
human automaton: the counterfeit human, a mechanical double
built on the principles of the clock, which even had ambitions to
play chess. As a courtier or simply as human company, the analogy

produces its effects through the play on the difference between representation and nature. The problem of the soul could well be posed in a new way in these conditions (on the terrain of fundamental Cartesian problems). But compare this with the industrial robot, which belongs to a completely different (second) order of simulation. Here problems of efficiency and function are dominant, since the robot is not only produced but belongs fundamentally to a different order of productivity and work. There is no longer any attempt to play with a representation of human forms, it is the efficient technical logic of operations alone which counts. The logic of the machine takes off from the world of analogy of forms. The hegemony of the machine as a mode of 'dead labour' commences its rule over living labour. This monumental overturning of previous frameworks, in which the dominance of the machine and the mode of production begins, is made possible only at the price of the elimination, in simulation, of any reference to living natural labour in order that a new generalized equivalence of abstract labour assert itself.

The predominant interpretation of capitalism, as a social order founded on a system of energies and forces of production, often identifies productivity with modernity itself. All such ideas are now open to question. It may well be, Baudrillard suggests, that 'production' was one of the first sectors of society to feel the impact of a new code: the code which effectively renders new systems of equivalences wherever it becomes established. In production it established the rule of mass production, of the unlimited production of identical objects. If this is the case, then capital is founded at a quite different level from that identified in traditional conceptions. It is located at the level of reproducibility, of the code of reproducibility. It is from this vantage point that it extends its dominance as a global system. Here the major intellectual pioneers are Walter Benjamin and Marshall McLuhan, he suggests, for they go beyond the point of taking productive forces at face value.[3] For this tradition of interpretation it is the code which is the structural medium, form, and principle of the new order. It no longer suggests that the form be adequate to the value of its input, but to that of its serial repetition (and by extension this applies to the nature of individuals in the labour force: not as human beings made into simple commodities, but as individuals become capable of being infinitely reduplicated.) In this way age-old human purposes are lost in serial repetition (1976: 100).

This second order of simulation in the world of mass productivity and work gives way to the third order at the point from which produced objects begin to be modelled not from a real basis but from an artificial nucleus of characeristics remote from forms of the counterfeit or the series (with its anchoring point in a conception of the authentic natural or useful 'real' object). Here the only point of connection which determines the order of simulation is the 'model' itself, now independent of any function or purpose arising out of a world of use. This is the world of the structural law of value, the dominance of reproducibility in a sense that is altogether different from the simple mass production. Here the model takes the place of the 'real', the referent, and becomes the 'signifier of reference' (1976: 100): the point from which internally differentiated modulations in the object are reproduced.

The principal ways of thinking about this are established in genetic biology and information theory: 'digitality is its metaphysical principle (the God of Leibniz) and DNA is its prophet' (1976; 1983f: 103). Phenomena, in this problematic, are generated from the model and its internal system of relations controlled cybernetically. The 'new operational configuration' is dominated by the control mechanism of the question and response process. From this point, Baudrillard argues, and thus catches the incautious in a feint, not only are all the old questions of repression and deviation ruled out of court, but so too are all differences between the real and the apparent. Second order signs that were 'crude, dull, industrial, repetitive' give way to an order of control that is buried 'in the depth of the "biological" body' – in 'black boxes where all the commandments ferment' (1976; 1983f: 104). From the theatre of the body, we have now entered, he argues, the era of cellular programming, of molecular emission of signals. In order to grasp the current system of social relations all analysis has to catch up with this displacement. The displacement he invokes here is an absolute one which erases all other formations in a flash, since he has no formal conception of social complexity at this level. But if there are considerable problems, there may also be some surprising gains worth looking for.

In this new order, scientific research is redoubled to find the smallest indivisible cell. But it soon becomes apparent that the code itself (which then becomes totally delirious) is not governed by a superior code of higher meaning. There is no purpose or meaning at all at this cellular level. The random combination of elements is all that is ever recognized as effective. All open space has disappeared, there are no gaps. This world is not even of one dimension. It is, he suggests, like the reflex world of a person gone crazy 'with solitude and repetition'. There is no aura around the object: everything (already?) is a combinatory ripe for decoding. The essential ambience of this world is the binary combination; the mode of decoding it through the zero and the one (0/1). In essence, the principal thinker of this order, Jacques Monod, says Baudrillard, has undertaken a dramatic recapitulation and updating of the Jesuit project, and in social theory all organicist imagery must be reconstructed in the light of genetic programmes. The immediate consequences, if all constraints are removed, concern the obvious elimination of the dialectic as a principle and with it the possibility of prophecy: everything must submit, it appears, to the principle of indeterminacy and randomness.

This new order of simulation, in Baudrillard's theory, puts an end, at a stroke, to all the heroic and Promethean concepts associated with industrial civilization: man, progress, and history. Yet paradoxically it moves to even higher levels of manipulation, ending all myths of the origin of society and meaning (in God) and all values based on an appeal to the real world and to nature (except as nostalgia: Monod often appears to appeal to the existence of a real world, to a principle of reality that humans seem incapable of going without, yet his work is dominated by the insistence on the internal hermetic sphere of genetic indetermination as a basic fact). It also puts an end, if all other forces and developments are ignored, which is what Baudrillard proposes, to the myth of revolutionary praxis and to the Revolution, as incompatible with a simulation order which has abolished human potentialities. At this point the ultimate violence of capital emerges as it becomes its own myth as an interminable aleatory machine leaving no possibility of reversal (1976; 1983f: 112), Baudrillard having eliminated all intermediary or countervailing structures. But then this is extreme thinking, which makes integral demands. If materialist theory is correct, Baudrillard will find a 'reality principle' somewhere. He proceeds to apply a fatal logic to a single structural principle. The result is a contradiction in terms, a transgression without a norm. His concepts are also located at a strategic level where important distinctions needs to be maintained. For example the 'models' in biological science are not created by fiat, as if the whole system had literally become ideal, but are the subject of formidable methodological constraints (unlike his own method).

THE EFFECTS OF THE THIRD ORDER OF SIMULATION
IN THE SPHERE OF POLITICAL CULTURE

The results and techniques of the sciences feed into the flow of social life. One important effect is the spread of the technique of digitality – in the form of the question and response (pre-coded): here all content is reduced to the question and answer format, even though it is not directly linked to the genetic order itself. It conforms to the same order of indeterminacy as the code, as if the chain of the code had been dismantled and its parts had become free-floating elements. It is the world of trial/error, of the personality test, of the referendum, of functionality in life through a reduction of everything to the yes/no. It is as though 'the entire system of communication has passed from that of a syntactically complex language structure to a binary sign system' (1976; 1983f: 116–17). As everything is pre-structured, social life becomes formed into a continuous stream of tests. These are always found to be 'perfect forms of simulation' and the ideal instruments for the conjuring of a new substance, public opinion. This substance is not, however, like the old abstract essences which were formed in relation to systems of imagined real or natural worlds. This order goes beyond this into the order of hyperreality itself: effectively the real world, its otherness, has been left behind as an idea appropriate to a different way of thinking. The intrusion of the binary schema, the 0/1, the yes/no, question/response, begins, effectively and dramatically, to render, immediately, every discourse inarticulate. It crushes the world of meaningful dialogue, of representation, of the formulation of questions which may be difficult, even impossible to answer: a golden age of discourse based on the play of real and appearance is abolished. From now on the media determine 'the very style of montage, of decoupage, of interpellation, solicitation, summation' (1976; 1983f: 123). Contrary to all expectations, as McLuhan alone has pointed out, says Baudrillard, this new age is not visual but tactile; everywhere it is the test, the pre-structured interrogation, that is the manipulator and formulator of the new consciousness.

   The effects on the political sphere are immediate and decisive, and it is necessary to allow Baudrillard full scope to develop these theses. It can be seen that the first serious result of this action by the mass media is the creation of universal suffrage. Here social exchange is reduced to its most essential function: to obtain an answer. But the context so created is also binary. This appears to establish a fundamental complicity between the code and the tendency to bipartite political rivalry. Political opinion polls effect and mirror alternations of the parties. As these polls are located beyond institutional supports the tendency inevitably becomes one in which opinion feeds on, and reproduces, itself. Public opinion is not produced, and it does not appear, in the era of production proper. It belongs to the order of simulation where reproduction predominates, where all opinions become interchangeable, all theories and political hypotheses become reversible, since it is a feature of the system at this point that questions are fundamentally undecidable. At first this is veiled, since scientific statistics give the illusion of solid content. It soon becomes evident, however, that public opinion is a 'fabulous fiction'. The effect of this is, he holds, absolutely decisive for modern society in all its aspects through the death of politics through the constant intervention of binary opposition: all political discourse is thoroughly drained of content. This is the outcome of the manipulation of the political by the politicians. Finally, political opinion polls retain meaning only for politicians and political scientists as these polls have only a tactical value for political manipulators. The mass media involved here bring into existence an 'operational simulation' of an informed political mass – (Baudrillard omits the caveat, if everything else is withdrawn from the scene).

This leads to a basic proposition: this form of simulation explains why public opinion in a modern democracy does not tend towards a single party. Indeed one-party states are genuinely unstable in comparison. The strange paradox is that all the immense effort made to reproduce public opinion ends up in societies that are 'puffed up on mere wind' (Baudrillard 1983f: 130). As this 'hot air' is entirely circular and tautological it can be seen as the ironic vengeance of the polled and the tested. The masses respond with a magnificent and triumphant vengeance of complete nullity in which the power structures are mirrored. In the end it is true to say that the end of representation is brought about by the representatives who manipulate and control the responses so well as to leave no remainder. Power is interred by the powerful. Thus a curious process of stabilization begins at the same time as the homogenization of the political élite at a level inevitably always concealed by the action of party alternation. In single-party systems the essential play in the system and its vital feedback processes are absent and public opinion, if it exists, cannot be manipulated. In the dual system, against all expectation again, representation ends as the law of equivalence of value, stemming from the code, begins to exercise its effectiveness: the inevitable to and fro motion begins, and from that moment, a public consensus is formed and re-formed. It is massaged into shape by pre-structured polls, so that after a period of time the distribution of votes tends to approach a natural split of 50/50 on each side: 'it is as if everyone voted by chance, or monkeys voted' (1976; 1983f: 132). The play of the polls takes over, and the process of representation, he says, becoming himself a monkey of a different sort, becomes outmoded. Even in the earlier period, voting implied and effected a certain degree of homogenization, but real antagonism existed and persisted. Today inner contradiction and differentiation in the voting mass tend to be eliminated and the outcome is the simulated play of opposition, interchange, and levelling of political opposition: 'the reversibility of entire discourses one into the other'. This extreme formulation, he says, seems at first sight perverse, yet it is clear that the tendency is undeniable. Thus against the idea of the duel, of a real struggle for power between distinct oppositional camps, in the new order reproduced political positions have to find their basis on the plane of value (here defined as that consensus which makes all difference at once non-difference).

More dramatically, Baudrillard argues, this tendency to duopoly exists also at the level of international relations. Here the control of world politics is in the hands of two superpowers and this rests on the equilibrium or balance of terror. This alone permits the development of a regulation and control of oppositions to be established. Superpower strategy does not principally concern atomic war, it concerns the establishment of a regulated structure of global relations. Here the mechanism of simulation again is in evidence in the binary scansion. The question however is why Baudrillard does not provide some counter cases, which would strengthen his case. His own argument *ad absurdum* weakens his position, but then his own theory has pronounced that dialogue is obsolescent.

THE HYPERREAL AND AESTHETICIZATION

This discussion leads Baudrillard to consider the hyperreal in more detail. It is not a form of the surreal which still plays with the existence of the real and requires it for its own effects. The distinction between the real and its representation begins to be effaced. In some cases this starts off from a reproduction of the 'real' in another medium, but as it passes from medium to medium the real is 'volatized' out of its former apparent solidity. It becomes hyperreal and hallucinatory. Out of the crisis of representation the *hyperreal* has had to be connected to repetition, first in relation to a reproduction of reality, but as reproducibility is established as dominant it ceased to require this support. This changes the whole cultural relation to the object, for example, as exemplified in modern literature, where objectivity is gradually disengaged from the object itself. This represents the end of metaphor and metonymy and the end of complex cultural syntax, in favour of a gaze which sweeps over objects without seeing in them anything other than their objectness. In this new order the new seductions of solicitation and passive involvement can be recognized as the manipulation of a 'joyous feedback' instituted in a new ecology of operationalized needs and desires. Leisure centres set up total environments, with the requisite complement of a new ambience (Baudrillard 1983f: 140).

Hyperreality entails the end of depth, perspective, relief: these are always to be found in the domain of subjective experience bound up with the human perceiver. The molecular code however insinuates here a new objectivity, and an associated optic. There are four forms of vertigo which can be identified here, says Baudrillard. First, the vertigo of the detail (hyperreal art), which loses itself in the particular. This is intensified in the mirror of the elaborately, hyper-detailed form where the real appears to feed on itself. But, third, the vertigo of the series is more important here, as established for example in the work of Warhol: a death is realized in the infinity of reproduction derived from the model. And, finally, it is solicited in the omnipresent binary coding of minimal differences. In this form, which can be seen in a contemporary genre of hyper-painting in which what counts is the frame, the border is the only remainder of the difference between the work of art and the wall it hangs on. Thus the definition of the real in this phase is that which cannot be reproduced, or for which there is 'no equivalent reproduction', and which must belong therefore to a nostalgic form of simulation or to an order which is not simulation (the symbolic). The *hyperreal* is the simulation form which dominates, and as such defines itself in relation to that which is always already reproduced.

This displacement has serious consequences, he argues. The crucial one is a general aestheticization of life, as everything falls under the sign of art which nevertheless, and paradoxically, loses all content. 'Art' penetrates to the very heart of the simulation process, but in the form of a psychosis: in another extreme provocation he argues that from now on nothing is repressed. The reality principle and the pleasure principle are displaced by the power of the principle of simulation. Yet this is not realized in the form of a hot, fevered, and fantastic world like that of surrealism. *Hyperrealist* art itself is cool, radically disenchanted, realized in the euphoria of the disappearance of cause and effect, beginning and end:

> analogous to the effect of distantiation internal to the dream, that makes us say we are only dreaming, but this is only a game of censure and of perpetuation of the dream, hyperrealism is made an integral part of a coded reality which it perpetuates.
>
> (Baudrillard 1976; 1983f: 147)

Modern art even in its *hyperreal* forms is no longer critical or transcendental: it colludes.[4]

This modernity which appears to promise unlimited development paradoxically comes to suppress change while permitting it in the oscillations of fashion.

Chapter 8

Fashion, the body, sexuality, and death

death has become incurable deviance

Baudrillard

During the mid-1970s, Baudrillard continued to broaden and deepen the analysis of the transformations, or, better, exorbitations, in crucial spheres of modern life under the impact of simulation processes. One key discussion focused on the meaning of fashion in this new context. This is an important continuation of reflections established in an earlier period and developed now in relation to his new conception of the structural law of value and how it invades modern cultures at every level. It specifies four processes which develop unequally but simultaneously: a movement towards the adoption of models and their simulation, in which there is, second, a differential play of elements, and in which, third, the elements become 'indifferent' to one another. Finally simulation is structured by the play of uniform values (equivalences made possible by the process of homogenization). All social spheres are affected by this process and one essential way in which this is achieved is through fashion: this is quite evident in clothes and consumer items, but it also begins to affect politics, science, and even sexuality. But lying even more deeply in the culture are crucial effects borne of the process of its formation. Adopting and extending Foucault's analyses of the genesis of modern forms of normalization, Baudrillard argues that the destruction of the symbolic modes of relating to death has meant that there is an unresolved problem of facing the dead in our societies, just as there is in facing the ill, the disabled, the criminal: contemporary societies cannot find a solution to the problem that they have themselves created – that the dead are dead.

But, first of all, take the problem of sexuality, he suggests. Once this passes into the realm of fashion there begins to develop a pattern of distinctive oppositions, and an immense system of fetishism begins to emerge, the object of both fascination and manipulation. This development involves a rupture in the culture, in the social imaginary, exactly at the moment when the new signs begin to alternate: it produces a kind of degrading and levelling of previous practices and values, a kind of general promiscuity of elements. It also sets off a resistance similar to that registered when sexuality falls into the realm of commodity exchange, but here it falls into the realm of fashion and signs: this results in a cool unrestrained sexuality freed from the previous system of boundaries and controls (Baudrillard 1976: 132).

But fashion, in its play of alternations, sets up its own cycles and rhythms. What is called modernity is therefore actually more complex than is usually thought. Since the Enlightenment there has been the gradual installation of linear and progressive time. But more than this: there has also been installed the specific cyclic time of fashion. The time of fashion has peculiar effects, as part of a number of processes which in the last resort are far more fundamental in their consequences, and with inverse outcomes, than those of simple progress: absence of change (and if there is progress, there is also, as we shall see, a point at which the linear escalation of effects can spiral out of control on the negative as well as the positive side). It introduces a particular version of the play of the new (modern) and the old (out of date), yet in the end the old is made into a resource and is recycled: in this way the new is rendered inoffensive. Modernity produces its own myth of the new which becomes part of the general effect of the play of the structural law of value on its elements: the emergence of distinctive oppositions, of a binary logic acting over cyclical time. This is the heart and essential character of fashion (which is the emblem) as a form of modernity (which is its code). It is clear, however, Baudrillard argues, that this world of fashion, modishness, trendiness, is quite different from a genuine order of ritual cycles. In fact, these two cycles are antagonistic, since the symbolic order will not admit this type of combinatory of equivalent elements to emerge as a system of alternations and does not permit its rituals to pass into the generalized field of pure, 'aesthetic' phenomena.

At this point Baudrillard returns to Roland Barthes for a consideration of the relation of fashion to the human body. Barthes suggests, in *The Fashion System* (1985), three distinct modalities, three ways in which there is a passage from an abstract to a real body. First, there is a pure form, without specific attributes; there is only abstract representation. For Barthes this is the simple model, the cover girl; she is both an individual yet completely caught in an institutional form which renders her body into no one's particular body, able, by a 'sort of tautology' to refer to the garment itself (Barthes 1985: 259). For Barthes the fashion magazine tends to present the cover girl in situation 'to unite with the pure representation of structure a rhetoric of gestures and poses meant to give a spectacularly empirical version of the body'. Here the event threatens structure. In the second case a certain kind of body or face is declared to be 'in fashion' (the model is still a fixed abstraction but circumscribed by season or year). The third solution gives to clothing the power to transform the body into the ideal body for fashion (it suggests the ability of fashion to submit event and any substance to its unlimited power of signification).

Baudrillard takes the opportunity to suggest that in fact Barthes' three forms can be seen to correspond to the actual historical evolution of the body in the regime of fashion: the initial models were not professional but gave way eventually to the mannequin. Today every (this particular exaggeration must be understood in its own right as Baudrillard's essential theoretical technique) woman has become a mannequin: each is summoned to treat her body as an investment through clothing and style. The fashion system of signification penetrates every way of relating to the body. The historical formation of fashion closely follows this order: in the early phases of capitalism it remained outside the artisan and peasant groups and was associated with marginal, or urban and foreign strata; in a second phase it began to penetrate and integrate all cultural signs as material production was integrated into political economy as the market became universal, but fashion was dominated specifically by the dominant cultural class. In the third phase fashion becomes a general way of life and no sphere escapes its logic: it has its own form of negativity (that which it defines as what it is to be not to be in fashion), becomes its own signified (as does production in the age of reproduction), and in the final state, just as it becomes universal, it disappears as a specific sphere; everything becomes fashion.[1]

One basic effect of this is a change in the relation to the unclothed body. In primitive societies, the body is painted and decorated. This is meaningful and structured in an exchange system and does not have a specifically aesthetic fashionableness. When the system of fashion begins to invade this terrain, the symbolic order of such meanings is abolished. It even brings about a new instrumental use of the naked body to induce a sexual tactics around nudity (a new pattern of simulation of the body). This changes above all the precise meaning and value of the female body itself in the culture. The irony is that the 'liberation' of fashion is also the moment of the 'liberation' of women. It is only quite recently that the body has been increasingly sexualized in its repression. This is both recent and is already beginning to change, its work done. The body, however, in this repressed form is the site of the action of signs of the fashion system; relieved of these elements the body is a model without attributes. Fashion has become modern sexuality in the sense that it has the function of establishing these qualities or attributes. As everything gets drawn into this system gradually all culture is affected by this specific sexual character, not sex itself but sexualization; by an inverse movement sex itself is influenced by this new sexualization of all spheres, unique to our culture. As it is the feminine body which is the emblem of this process, women's liberation is caught up in it. Following Foucault's own exemplary analysis of madness (which he turns into a fundamental process of the formation of the modern world) he suggests that, as women leave their traditional seclusion, society is itself feminized. It is as if, like proletarians, liberated only to be a labour force, women are liberated as a 'force' for pleasure, for fashion:

From the moment women enter the world of work like everyone else, on the model of the proletariat, all the world enters the world of emancipated sex and fashion, on the model of women.
(Baudrillard 1976: 149)

In this case it can be seen that if the worker is separated from himself in the process of exploitation under capitalism, women are separated from themselves and their own bodies under the sign of beauty and the pleasure principle.

Here a major problem confronts all revolutionary opposition in relation to fashion. It is a very specific kind of code: all internal forms of negativity can be absorbed and dealt with on its own grounds. There is no internal lived articulation of contradiction: it is impossible to escape its own specific reality principle. Yet, despite appearances to the contrary, fashion and its alternations are caught within a repressive logic. Here again Baudrillard forces his conclusion to the limit by arguing that to resist the content of the code is only to obey its logic. 'It is the diktat of "modernity" ' (1976: 151). The only effective alternative lies

> in a deconstruction of the sign-form of fashion and of its very principle of signification, just as the alternative of political economy lies perhaps only in the deconstruction of the commodity form and of the very principle of production.
>
> (1976: 151)

Yet this, however radical, violently contradicts his own extreme positions, which would suggest that even these efforts would become part of the code. The temptation in this mode of analysis is to find implacable and unilateral escalations in each individual site (yet everything stays the same): every culture has a single principle and every object a single essence. Baudrillard thinks this is the nature of the world, or at least in the analyses of this particular period which reverse those of his early writings. Yet there are important exceptions, such as the analysis of the Beaubourg building which I examine in a later chapter, and which, paradoxically, could not have been written had not Baudrillard developed these extreme, pataphysical positions in pure abstraction.

SEXUALITY

More and more the 'body' is made, under these circumstances, itself into a new system, rather like the object system: it becomes subject to a new discipline of signs and the exchange between signs. In this system, Baudrillard proposes, the general basis of exchange is a specific fetishization of the phallus, and the staging of castration effects. The whole logic of the process can be regarded as a close parallel to the general process of political economy, in producing value interchanges. As the process in this sphere extends itself, what occurs is the generalized evocation of erection and castration in fashion, advertising and even in striptease itself (1976: 155). As the same elements are found throughout, there is no doubt, he claims, that these form a single system: it is one which could be called in Freudian terms a perverse eroticism. Principally, he suggests, there is a replaying through parody of castration as the symbolic articulation of a lack: the bar of the censor has the structural form of articulating two full terms. The terrain is not an erogenous zone, but the attempt is made to produce an erotic zone where one element is raised to the level of a signifier of the phallus: this is simplified into a pure term of the sexual. The erotic comes, eventually, to be that which is placed under the bar. Unlike all previous symbolic representations of sexuality, here the woman's body itself takes on the role of the erotic and it becomes phallic.

Thus, although the body does not in itself naturally distribute the terms masculine and feminine in a rigid division, the body is a basis from which symbolism can be abstracted, particularly a castration symbolism: the foot of a Chinese woman can be mutilated and then venerated. The system of signs and marks forms a system which has to be interpreted. Take lipstick and make-up in the modern system. The intensively made-up mouth is not directly functional (it is not a sexual orifice). It is a sign, an erotic jewel, and therefore a sign-value. It enters into the system of exchanges, here of tumescence or erection. It is, in transference, the desire of man in his own image (erection). The sexual act now, he argues, is often only possible on condition that the woman is converted into a phallic object and is available to be caressed as a phallus. This is consistent with the formation of a political economy of desire in which the basic term is the phallus and the exchange system works in relation to exchanges into and out of this value. The body of the woman is unveiled in a thousand variations. This is a new form of simulation under the frame of the law of phallic value. The phallus thereby functions in the form of a fetish, renewed without cease by the work of symbolic castration effects.

Ironically, it is the body of the woman which is the privileged site of this drama, both for men and for women. It is the woman's body which has come to play the role of the general equivalent of the phallus (because, he says, for certain it does not have one). The man's body carries the 'true mark', which valorizes the system as a whole. It is thereby not available to play the role of demarcation which can be done only through its derivatives. There is a strict bar on the availability of the image of the erect male member (no advertising can reveal it or exploit it directly). Representation of the erect penis is controlled, and transferred to the body of the woman. Thus the position of woman should not be understood as an aliena-tion for there is no primary sexual basis for the social alienation of women as conceived in humanist writings. It is more a question of domination, since women, in their very bodies, are annexed to the phallic order. As this generalizes itself the operation of its effects and its bar condemn women, on all other planes, to non-existence. (No mistake should be made, he reflects, by comparing make-up with primitive masks. In a primitive society the mask plays a function in the symbolic exchange between persons and gods, and is located within the practice of the group. It is is not the individual who behind the mask manipulates the situation in order to negotiate the creation of an identity. The idea of fetishism does not apply to the primitive; it applies only to our culture.)

It is instructive, he suggests, to analyse the good and the bad striptease in modern culture. The good striptease does its work as the slow action of a discourse which cannot produce all its terms at once: it is cool and reveals a mastery over the evocation of the body through disrobing. The striptease, though this seems bizarre, in its disrobing actually adds signs to the body in order to produce the body as an effigy of the phallus: it assumes the form of an erection of the body. That is why direct nudity itself as a body denuded of signs destroys such an erotic objective, which is what happens in the bad striptease. The first brings into play an intense mirror of rigorous narcissicism which reduplicates the equivalent movements, through a panopoly of signs and gestures, of the erection of the body – and this is why it is reduplicated in all codes (make-up, fashion, advertising, etc.). Instead of thinking that the striptease artist makes love to the audience (a popular misconception, he notes) the striptease is always indirect and works essentially as a narcissicism. This is a veritable work of transubstantiation, he suggests, not of bread and wine, but of body and phallus. It does not aim for the truth of the naked body, despite all appearances, but in the opposite direction, towards the body's envelopment in the exchange system of signs. This effects the true castration of women (and indirectly of men):

> to be castrated is to be covered with phallic substitutes. Woman is covered in them, and is summoned to make a phallus of her body if she is ever to be desirable.
>
> (1976: 168–9)

At the same time, the striptease artist, over and above making this transformation, evolves and adopts a certain type of fixed gaze. It is usually interpreted as distantiation, a coolness which marks the boundaries of the erotic. But it is necessary to redefine the cool gaze of the 'good' striptease as that of the mannequin and therefore of a certain quality of modern culture itself. It is the gaze of autoeroticism, of the object-woman who looks at herself as perfection and perversion. Woman is never so seductive as when she adores herself, he suggests. Around the mannequin is an intense narcissism, a paradigm of self-seduction.[2] The woman becomes her own fetish and, therefore, a fetish for the other.

The striptease is thus in effect a spectacle of castration, and best understood through the question of narcissicism and its relation to social control. This is no longer a simple narcissism, but one which works through a cultural sophistication, a manipulation of signs and values. The new political economy of values in this realm is founded on a destructuration of the elements of the system and restructuring of the forms and locations of investments. It is a 'reappropriation' of the body in terms of new models and structures. From now on, narcissicism becomes part of a manipulable system. This is made possible by the enticement, the interpellation, of the new subject of the narcissicistic system who is no longer the familiar 'I' of previous systems. Now it is the 'you' of the advertisement. The previous subject is now fragmented and 'personalized' and put into the (always already pre-coded) play of the system. This 'you' does not refer to any one individual, it is a simulation from a model and enables the discourse of the model to be conducted. It is in this sense, the ghost, the double of the code: 'The phantom which appears in the mirror of signs' (1976: 173).

Today's social liberation passes through a stage of narcissism (the only critical meaning, he suggests, of the notion of the 'mirror phase' today). Previously, the mirror phase was dominated by the law of the father, accompanied by the threat of violence. Today it has become a pacific, non-violent form of repression, and goes beyond the sexual division to control the symbolic order itself. As it does so it goes from the law of the father to the desire of the mother. In so far as the new system seeks to replace the incest taboo, a vital form in symbolic exchanges, and abolish it, the new system tends not just towards narcissism but to incestuous narcissism. Fetishistic perversion results from a desire for the mother and never leaves the circle of desire. The traditional order accomplishes, if it is successful, the word of the father. But the perverse subject accomplishes the desire of the mother, and remains within the family: it not surprising to find here new qualities and characteristics emerging in the subject, not so much those of neurosis and hysteria associated with puritanical repression, but obsession and anxiety, as society becomes permissive and gratificatory. The subject becomes a marionette of the mother's desires.

On the basis of a recognition of this fundamental change, all revolutionary perspectives must transform themselves. Between the law of the father and the desire of the mother, between repression and transgression, regression and manipulation, a way out must be found, he says, through a form of the symbolic. For symbolic exchange is itself founded on the cancellation of value: it is 'neither regression of the law (towards incest) nor pure and simple transgression (always dependent on law) – it is the resolution of that law' (1976: 176).

The question is to what extent does this analysis itself convert one discourse into another? As Baudrillard himself tries to think through the effects of homogenization, the problem of the critical separation between discourses becomes acute. In a sense there is a convenient escape route for Baudrillard: these various discourses, sociology, Marxism, psychology, themselves reflect a world which is dramatically constraining its discourses into one formal language. He merely reflects this. On the other hand, he has made a violent attack on Foucault and Deleuze, arguing that their analyses can convert one into another; if this occurs, he says: forget them (Baudrillard 1987c).

DEATH AS ABNORMALITY

Yet these analyses remain for Baudrillard at a superficial level, for they still do not get to the root of things. Beyond the question of sexuality there is another which affects even more profoundly the fate of the body: death. The central and crucial chapters of *L'Echange Symbolique* attempt to construct a genealogy of death in the gradual emergence of culture out of symbolic orders. Many, even Baudrillard's detractors, have acknowledged that this analysis is remarkable.[3] Where there have been many attempts to establish genealogies of morals (Nietzsche), of capital (Marx), of punishment (Durkheim and Foucault), even of time (Debord), Baudrillard has possibly the right to claim to have located one that is more basic. Baudrillard notes that this genealogy is similar to Foucault's consideration of madness, but articulates it with a conception of death in societies dominated by symbolic reversibility (as indicated by Debord) which turns the discussion towards an explicit critique of modern communism (1976: 225). The principle of the genealogy traces the gradual process of exclusion, the extradition, of the dead from society; little by little the dead cease to exist, and death becomes a state of abnormality. Baudrillard follows the analysis to the conclusion that, paradoxically, in consequence our culture is a culture of death: by abolishing that which cannot be abolished death makes its symptomatic mark everywhere.

Baudrillard's analysis traces the path of the dead. At first, in primitive societies they are held in the village.[4] The dead are later ghettoized on the outskirts of the village, and then they disappear altogether and cease to exist as beings in society. Even the mad and the delinquent are received in society at some point, but the dead are never received as such. It is not any longer normal to be dead and this is new. 'Death has become incurable deviance.'[5] The situation is altogether different in primitive societies where there is no concept of purely biological death, or more accurately the notion of birth or death as a purely physical process is without meaning. It is even more powerful than this formula suggests, since everything that cannot be symbolically exchanged is a danger to the group. It can be suggested, says Baudrillard, that what for us occurs in the biological realm comes to exist in our imaginary, but in primitive societies everything occurs in the symbolic.

One way of approaching this problem is to examine the process of initiation. One stage of initiation, as in all rites of passage, involves ritual death in order that a rebirth may occur. In primitive societies there is an exchange between ancestors and the living, a direct contact between the dead and the living. Thus, instead of the absolute caesura which exists in our own society between birth and death ritual there is an evident and strong social relationship: reciprocal exchange, a form of the cycle of gift and counter-gift. It is quite remote in principle from any idea of life or death as chance or random events. In primitive society exchange is therefore conceived as reversible, in our own it is conceived as irreversible (1976: 203). Because of this there is no formal opposition or irreconcilability between life and death in primitive societies. And this has other consequences, he argues, for this is how the incest taboo should be understood: in our society it no longer functions to permit exchange between the living and the dead. And if the term revolution retains any meaning, he insists it 'can only consist in the abolition of the separation of death, not of equality in survival' (1976: 200).

Baudrillard's argument is important here for the shaping of much of his subsequent theorizing, so it is essential to present the crucial propositions. Baudrillard's point of departure is the parallel between the genealogy of death and the evolution of normalization processes. Madness itself, he argues, is never only the line of partition between the sane and the mad, this line of demarcation is shared between the two sides, and it is in relation to this shared line that sanity defines itself. A society which incarcerates its mad is a society profoundly invested in madness, and which in turn valorizes sanity. The effects of the long centuries of work done by 'madness' on society, as a work of discipline, are complete, and the asylum now has a different aspect, its walls have been breached. Not, he notes, by growing tolerance, but because the process of normalization has been effective, at the cost of generalizing a kind of madness throughout society: 'madness has become ambient' (1976: 197). There is a new absorption of the asylum back into the heart of the society, where, he argues, normality has become so refined that it resembles madness, the virus has passed to all the sites and fibres of normal existence.

Baudrillard argues that exactly the same processes have occurred in relation to the dead. Death is, in the last analysis, the line of social demarcation which separates the dead from the living, and it affects each side equally. But the logic of symbolic exchange is indestructible, and re-establishes the equivalence of life and death in the fatality of survival, for this is where death finds its home in repression, as life is a survival determined by the power of death. This fact is hidden from view by Enlightenment ideology, as developed and codified by writers such as Comte, who have argued that it is in the progression of the stages of culture from animism, polytheism to monotheism that the notion of the soul became disengaged and transformed into metaphysical entity and which could be abolished in secular criticism (though obviously Comte had difficulties with this). For Baudrillard, on the other hand, the notion of the soul and immortality is a route to the investigation of power. His starting point is the very Durkheimian assumption that in societies where there is a current and living exchange between the living and the dead, where there is reciprocity, reversibility, there is no necessity for the dead to be immortalized. This would, in fact, have the effect of breaking the cycle of symbolic intercourse. The 'extradition' of the dead, their exclusion, is accompanied, when it arrives, by the increasing power of the soul. This gradually becomes immortal, and measures by this fact the degree to which symbolic exchange has broken down. It measures the extent to which the dead have been expelled from the midst of society — into exile. Immortality is a strange idea, he remarks. It extends a limited life into an eternal one, while at the same time, as a social phenomenon, it democratizes itself in the social mass, after having been the limited right of the powerful. This is a recent transformation in world historic perspective. It can be traced in Egypt, for example, where it began as a process limited to kings, then gradually embraced high priests, leaders, the rich, and the main figures of the dominant class. The remainder of society were left the right to their death and their double. About 2000 BC, he remarks, each individual acceded into immortality, in a kind of social conquest. ('One can imagine', he reflects, 'the revolts and social movements which developed the demand for the right to immortality for all' (1976: 198).) This reveals that the question of the soul, and the death of the soul, was from the beginning a question of power. It too can be constructed into the genealogy: first, a stage where there is a limited, a relative soul, since there is no political structure; second, immortality was generalized in the period of the great despotic empires; the kings and the gods were promoted into this new sphere, followed by immortality for each individual. There is a conjunction between the growing abstraction of power as a force in the great empires, and it is notable that Christianity converted this abstraction in its own way whereas the Greeks had not attained this degree of universality and their gods remained mortal. Even at the beginning of Christianity not all questions here had been resolved, and the death of the soul was still a possibility.

   But Christianity is characterized by a strong democratic element; everyone is, theoretically, equal before death. This remains, however, largely part of the mythology of Christianity itself. In effect this relation was always dependent on the contemporary definition of the human, and it was convenient to exclude primitives, women, children, from the category, as also the mad, criminals, and others. In effect, it is the powerful who have souls; there is an actual inequality before death, which makes the soul a reflection in its turn of the power differences in society. The powerful have a right to immortality, the others to punctual death, and nothing has changed, much, he suggests, since the despotic empires. The same temptations and traps are found here as they were in the past: the trap of the demand for the immortality of the soul, in parallel with the demand for the equal allocation of objects. This results from and contributes to the splitting up of the social body, and serves no purpose for the revolutionary. Immortality in this form depends on a general equivalent bound to a process of linear time, to abstraction, to accumulation. There is no way out here.

It may be possible, he implies, *to regard the social process of death as itself a social ideological apparatus (dispositif, (1976: 200)), one of the first great ideological apparatuses of the state.* It seems that the priests were well able to develop strategies of the control of sacrifices, in other words a strategy to attempt to prohibit death, and in so doing successfully to disconnect the articulations of the previous cycles, preventing the possible play of reversibility. It breaks the unity of the living and the dead, and the exchange between them. It is a first order, fundamental technique of social control, for control over the dead acts more effectively than any other. The dead are placed under surveillance, and are locked up. These conclusions, he notes, are Kafkaesque: the fundamental law is established and power is maintained by the guardians at the gate to death. In this conception, social and individual repression is not generated in relation to the subject's drives, it is the repression of the dead, of death, which rebounds back to haunt repressive socialization (1976: 200).

Effectively, then, social control is exercized at the pole of death and relations with the dead. The dead occupy a primary reserved domain, guarded by priests who control, through structures of obligatory mediations, exchanges with the dead. It is at the gate, the barrier, where power is set up, and it feeds on all the other separations which follow this initial one, the separation between life and death. In the end this apparatus of death, the immortal, comes to weigh heavily on the living, just as dead labour comes to weigh down on living labour. The living become residual survivors to power (the dead). Reflect again on the story of the student at Prague, he suggests, the pact with the devil is a pact with death, a pact with political economy. The devil can be considered, in this story, a hostile double of the subject, yet in the form where 'death takes its revenge' (Baudrillard 1976: 201). Death, which can never be abolished, now enters into the objects of the mundane world; the soul is lost in an unequal exchange with the devil (the hostile double). Evil then is found at this level of negativity, menace, deathly forces, which have escaped the action of group exchange, of symbolic intercourse, based on a degree of equality of reversibility. These hostile doubles, the immanence of errant forces (ibid.: 219), turn back, as persecutors, on the subject, who is thrown into the effect of the uncanny (Freud's *'unheimliche'*).[6]

In the world established after the disintegration of the traditional Christian and feudal communities of the Middle Ages by bourgeois reason and political economy, each individual is alone before death. Political economy is a massive attempt to accumulate against death, but it is caught in the irony that accumulation is death. This cannot resolve itself dialectically but enters into a deadly spiral. The culture becomes one in which there is an immense effort to dissolve the difference between life and death, to conjure away the ambivalence of death to the single profit of reproduction of life as value. The phantasy which predominates is the aim of abolishing death itself, and this has striking pathological effects throughout all the social separations of our societies, in religion as the desire for eternity, in science as the desire for eternal truth, and in production as the desire for infinite accumulation (1976: 225).

It is important, following this discussion, he notes, to clarify the difference between two kinds of utopian notions. One is simple, and demands the end of all separations with a fusion of all elements so that alienation is brought to a final conclusion. This is, he says, a naive utopia, based on the dream of the original whole. The second conception is not nostalgic, but revolutionary, and demands, in the present, the ending of these separations in the formidable play of reversion of life and death.[7] This is a basic clarification of the active utopianism in Baudrillard, which is linked to his tactic of outbidding, provocation, and forcing arguments to their extreme.

Chapter 9

Anagrammatic resolutions

The orphic dispersion
Baudrillard

SAUSSUREAN THESES

The great appeal of the poetic for Baudrillard is not simply in the intrinsic qualities of literature and the sublime in its art, it is also as a demonstration in practice of forms of symbolic, non-accumulative cultural processes. A good example, he suggests, is the good butcher (Chuang-tzu, referenced to volume three of *The Principles of Hygiene* (Baudrillard 1976: 187)). Unlike the bad butcher, he does not waste, or dull, his knives. The body is not, for him, a system of functionally juxtaposed positive organs like a functional syntax. The good butcher proceeds anagrammatically, that is, he works between two levels of text: manifest and latent. The good butcher follows, by his skill, 'the body under the body', as its anagram which is dispersed in it.[1] The knife follows the articulation of the one below the other. This other is different from a simple anatomical system of connections, and as the knife follows it is a work of art which establishes a resolution. This can be taken as a way of thinking of the relationship of the effectiveness of the symbolic in primitive societies: it is not a kind of magic, but always a question of anagrammatic resolution. Its aim is only the resolution of the signifier 'in the orphic dispersion of the body' and of the rhythm of the knife which follows the dispersion of the anagram and resolves it (1976: 189).

This appears highly mysterious, but it refers specifically to the theses developed by Saussure in his many notebooks on anagrams in classical poetry of antiquity and beyond. These notebooks were made available in part in a short work by Jean Starobinski in 1971, and Baudrillard was quick to argue that they represent not just a challenge to modern linguistics but also to Saussure's own mature structural linguistics of the sign. They are for Baudrillard a fundamental discovery which has important implications across all theories of language and culture. They concern the possibility of a language without repression, beyond the laws, axioms, and vision of orthodox linguistics. This is the terrain of the symbolic exchange in language.

These discoveries of Saussure are announced as having been established around the implied rules of construction of ancient literature, Latin poetry (and beyond). The rule or law of coupling (*couplaison*), and that of the theme-word (*mot-theme*):

A. The law of coupling involves i) in these works of poetry a vowel has the right to exist only if there is a counter-vowel at some point in the verse. If there is an even number of syllables the vowels must couple exactly, and must always in the end leave: zero. ii) The same is true for consonants, and no less strict, there is always an even number one for each consonant. iii) If there is a remainder or residue, in verses that are uneven, this residue will be repaired in the following verse.

B. The law of the theme-word involves the decomposition of the name of a god or hero into an anagram which is dispersed throughout the verses. It is, says Baudrillard, something like a votive offering, a dedication, the name to which and from which it is dedicated (1976: 287).

And these two rules can obviously coexist.

Very briefly Saussure finds the name Scipio in the following Latin line

Taurasi Cisauna Samio cepit.

It is, he says, an anagrammatic verse: ci + pi + io, plus the S from Samio.

Another anagrammatic verse (scipio) gives

Subigit omne Loucanam opsidesque abdoucit

and Saussure comments: here we find ouc ($\times$ 2), d ($\times$ 2), b ($\times$ 2), it ($\times$ 2), i ($\times$ 2), a ($\times$ 2), o ($\times$ 2), n ($\times$ 2), m ($\times$ 2). The principle residues are picked up in the subsequent verse.

The search for anagrams in Lucretius's *De Rerum Natura* is complemented by the establishment of a key formula which provides a 'mannequin' for the theme-word (for example Aphrodite), and this mannequin begins and ends with the first and last phonemes of the theme-word and in the best cases gives a good number of the phonic constituents (Starobinksi 1971: 79). An example:

> *Nam simul ac species patefactast uerna diei,*
> *et reserata uiget genitabilis aura fauoni,*
> *aeriae primum uolucres te, diua, tuumque*
> *significant initum perculsae corda tua ui.*

The mannequin here is, says Saussure, *Aeriae primum volucres te.* The syllables Saussure registers in a discussion as A (from the mannequin), AF (aureAFavoni 1.2), FR (? possibly a p as is the case in many anagrams, mannequin), ROD (given by cORDa, 1.4), DI (te DIva, 1.3), IT (inITum, 1.4), TE (mannequin). As well as the anagrammatic form itself, Saussure also refers to that of the anaphonic. The former is a perfect reproduction of the phonic elements of the theme-word, the latter is based on the assonance of the word which may be more or less present and repeated, that is, it may not form the totality of syllables of the word.[2]

At first sight, says Baudrillard, these rules appear rather insignificant, too restricted to account for the poetic effect. But if Saussure is understood properly the effect is one of the subversion of linguistics, for the law of the poem is that after its process there is nothing left. Instead of a process of accumulation of meaning, of value, the poetic involves the destruction of meaning and the annihilation of value. It cannot be understood by a framework of productivities, of poetry as a means or mode of poetic effects. Take the first law. On one reading the poetic can be regarded as a production of symmetries, of alliterative effects, or as the accumulation of effects of doubling, or as a mode of expressiveness of the poet or of representation of the world. For Saussure this is not at all what is at question here, which is rather the cyclical cancellation two by two of terms, an extermination through a cycle of redoubling. This goes for the second law as well. It is not an attempt to make the god reappear (as is erroneously implied by Starobinski (1971: 33)), it is not an attempt to re-totalize after having been alienated. It is the dispersion of the terms, the extermination of the name, without return. It is a sacrifice in the midst of the poem in the same way as an offering is made in the sacrificial ceremony at the end of which nothing is left over.

Thus to the order of linguistics and the signifier which revolves around the equivalence of the signifier and signified, the linearity of the signifying chain, and the unlimited production of effects through combination, the symbolic order of the poetic suggests the breaking of all three assumptions: the corpus is strictly limited not as a matter of penury, but as a structure in its own right; it is a basic law of the symbolic itself. In this sphere there is no general system of equivalences. Therefore the semiological system of linguistics which works on this assumption fails before it.

BAUDRILLARD'S POEMS

It is well worth noting here that Baudrillard himself is a poet and a collection of his poetry was published in 1978, entitled *L'Ange de Stuc*. (The poems are untitled beyond this and there are no page numbers, but it is clear that there are a number of identifiable sections, which can be id᷍ n ᷍fied (seventeen); only where absolutely essential in their semiolo᷍ ᷍al sense will they be translated here, since this kind of writing is aimed above all at that which is annulled with its own terms.) It can be suggested that these poems not only relate to these principles of the poetic as a symbolic exchange system, but also say this in so many words:

Absent on est comme
la voix dans l'aphonie
ou la maison inhabitée
parm᷍ la musique sourde
et les éclats de verre

(Baudrillard 1978a: section 9)

This is perhaps still at the level of signification, and can be translated, but, at the anaphonic level itself, this becomes impossible. For example in section five of *L'Ange de Stuc* we find the fragments of the sounds of Saussure and Mauss themselves scattered throughout:

Si les sentiers même
solubles par devers
l'absence de vent
sur l'eau où
elles chassent, et où
leur ressemblent
les bêtes qu'elles chassent . . .

>   – à l'image
> des autres, non de soi, et
> en irrealité des autres
> s'il le faut, mais
> hors de nous, toujours, vers où
> se réconcilient les forces
> centrifuges prises
> dans l'absurdité du paysage
> alors?
>
>   (Baudrillard 1978a: section 5)

One could easily suggest the first line as a mannequin for Saussure, and then the consonants and vowels, even words (ou × 2 and chassent × 2) begin to exterminate themselves around the au and the ur components of sau-ssure (eau/sur 1.4). And later it is possible to regard the mannequin for Mauss in the word MaiS (1.6 up), around which circle iMAge, AUtres, deSautres, or in the line 6 up, Mais, fAUt, S'il. But note also the possibility of Saussure in the second part here: S'il fAUt, abSURdite. In the final lines of this section we find

> rions par la déchirure
> oral au seuil de la
> démotion, car les méduses
> de la notion sont
> la volition médusées par
> la ruse des lignes brisées.
>
>   (ibid.)

The question arises as to what such a build up suddenly of r, d, b, of ar, ri, as well as o, means if not some hint perhaps that the name from whom the gift is dedicated is being presented in anaphoric form: b o d ri ar (Baudrillard)? But still note that the form of Ferdinand de Saussure is also possibly assonated in:

> r i ons de chir ure
> Ferdinand de Saussure

No doubt these are fanciful suggestions, especially in the light of Baudrillard's comment to the effect that these lines were written in the 1950s.[3] It is, however, important not to leave these poems at that point, for they deserve further consideration. What do they mean, or seek to achieve? The answer to this is to be found in Baudrillard's project to provide a theory and critique of the new forms of doubling in the culture of the Renaissance, what he has called the first order of simulation. This is certainly an attempt to provide a theoretical–poetic critique of these new forms of simulation, the baroque apocalypse, as is indicated in the epigraph:

Et ils virent un ange de stuc
dont les extrêmités se rejoignaient
dans une même courbe
(1978a: 2)

A poetic formulation which appears in the actual flow of the prose of *L'Echange Symbolique et la Mort* (1976: 81), where it is part of the discussion of the hegemonic principle of a closed homogeneous universe in one single substance.

But lines from these poems are also dispersed in Baudrillard's book *Seduction* (1979: 86–7), in a section entitled 'le Trompe l'oeil ou la simulation enchantée', which considers the changing experience of space in the Renaissance. The *trompe-l'oeil*, he says, seems to project a new space in front of itself. The eye is fooled by the apparent existence of interior space. An opaque mirror effect is thrown before the eye – the space of appearance properly conceived. Everything here is artefact. Objects are disconnected from their contexts. And actually there is no 'representation' of nature. The crucial consequence is that the horizontal disappears as horizon. The *trompe-l'oeil* is weightless, everything which appears is maintained in suspense (in light, time).

> If there is light it is mysterious, without origin, like stagnant water, water without depth, soft to the touch like a natural death. Here things have long since lost their shadows (their substance). Something other than the sun shines on them, a brighter star, without an atmosphere, or with an ether that doesn't refract. Perhaps death illuminates these things directly, and that is their sole meaning. These shadows do not move with the sun; they do not grow with the evening; without movement, they appear as an inevitable edging. Not the result of chiaroscuro, nor a skilful dialectic of light and shadow . . . they suggest the transparency of objects to a black sun.
> (Baudrillard 1990a: 62; cf. 1988b: 155–6)

The project in the poems is the evocation of these ideas in a different modality, that is, the evocation of the world as it, in Baudrillard's words, approaches 'the black hole from which, for us, reality, the real world, and normal time emerge' (1990a: 62). This deathly world appears in the poems:

Une horloge sans aiguille
impose le temps mais
laisse deviner l'heure
            (1978a: 10)

and in the text of *Seduction*: 'une horloge sans aiguille qui laisse
deviner l'heure' (1979: 86; 'a clock without hands that leaves one to
guess the hour' 1990a: 61). Or again,

L'eau est douce au toucher
comme une mort naturelle
            (1978a: 10)

and how it appears in the text of *Seduction* (1979: 86–7): 'cette
mysterieuse lumiere est comme . . . une eau sans profondeur, une
eau stagnant, douce au toucher comme une mort naturelle'.

Evidently this kind of relation between theory and poetry involves
Baudrillard's specific form of reversibility: he achieves a high
degree of reversion between the poetic (and its links with the
symbolic, as transfinite, untranslatable), and the semiological (as
finite). But what exactly is Baudrillard trying to evoke? It is
conceived, he says, in theoretical terms, as the decisive and catastrophic (the poetic invocation lives the eerie rending of the
symbolic world) moment of the emergence of western 'reality'. The
trompe-l'oeil is its ironic simulacrum (1990a: 64) (which has its
parallel in the twentieth century in the ironic delirium of surrealism
which plays with obsessive modern functionality). Baudrillard
comments: in both cases there is a metaphysical dimension for
'they seek out the wrong or the reverse side of things, and under-
mine the world's apparent factuality. This is why the pleasure they
give us, their seductiveness . . . is radical; for it comes from a
radical surprise borne of appearances, from a life prior to the mode
of production of the real world' (1990a: 64; and see 1983f: 147).

Baudrillard's ideas can be constituted from his disparate writings
on this problem. It is clear that one of the important issues is the
nature of the world the Renaissance displaced. It was never a world
of static oppositions or leaden attributes, but the oppositions, say
between water and fire, fire and earth, were attractive to each
other. Yet it was not a confused world, or one without order. What
is rarely grasped from a structuralist point of view, he argues, is
that these elements are distinct, attract, yet never fuse, because
their relations are those of the duel; they gravitate towards each

other agonistically. In the new world of the Renaissance *trompe-l'oeil* the universe of attraction is faltering, it is the collapse of seduction into ironic simulation, the effect of the black sun.

The key point was once reflected by Lévi-Strauss as the search for the 'possession of the object' in western art. The account given here in Baudrillard is certainly not psychological. It is rather the attempt to grasp this moment of the arrival of ironic realism, as the effect of

a sudden break in reality and the giddiness of feeling oneself fall. It is this loss of reality that the surreal familiarity of objects translates. With the disintegration of this hierarchical organisation of space that privileges the eye and vision . . . something emerges that . . . we express in terms of touch.

(1990a: 62–3)

L'eau est si claire
qu'on peut la faire saillir
par les bêtes.

Les muscles striés
innervent le sol
renversé. L'eau
même est innervée
de la teneur du mal.
Et rien n'est séparé.
Tout est exact comme
le sang sous les ongles.
Ainsi alternent
les choses imaginées
qu'entourent leur
propre vide, où luit
immergée comme
une chaise l'épée
gestuelle du
Soleil.
(1978a: section 4)

Chapter 10

Transpolitical objects

Things have found a way to elude the dialectic of meaning,
they did this by going to extremes

Baudrillard

THE CATASTROPHE

Baudrillard's next phase of writing attempted to follow the pure
logics of the 'object', placing these in a context of an analysis of
western culture having entered into a phase of excess, exorbitance,
for these objects have crossed a threshold, they are transsexual,
transaesthetic, transeconomic objects.[1] No doubt sociologists who
follow up these ideas will also conceive them as 'transsocial' objects
(Best and Kellner 1991). But Baudrillard cannot follow this route
since the concept of the social has already been developed in a completely different direction (the death of the social). For Baudrillard,
these are transpolitical figures in a society in which the social is no
longer a vital principle. (Note that this is not to say that society has
been dissolved; what has changed is the idea of a society with a
systematic overdetermined complexity, or a society in depth,
having a separated structure of economic basis and political,
cultural, and social spheres (the latter being the latest arrival and
the first to depart – according to Baudrillard)).

It is not as if the force of overdetermination has departed however. It is still useful to Baudrillard, but in a new form: each sphere
now, paradoxically, overdetermines itself (1987d: 30). But the
generic term is perhaps that of the transfinite: a term developed in
linguistic analysis out of set theory by Julia Kristeva, it indicates
that which has passed beyond the finite, which is thus 'more than' a

finite figure, but is not infinite. Kristeva wanted to use this term in relation to the difference between the sign (the finite relation of signifier and signified) and the symbol (which has a transfinite relation to its signifying field). Baudrillard however displaces the site of application from the theory of the symbol to that of the disappearance of the sign. In this way Baudrillard has hoped to reveal a specific characteristic of western culture, which he conceives in a neo-Durkheimian way as the emergence not only of anomic but also of anomalous disfiguration in the culture (that which afflicts its anatomy, in Durkheim's terms a teratology).[2] But these, theoretically defined disfigurations are experienced none the less, in the form of a liberation. This is the key paradox for Baudrillard, the emergence of liberation, as both, in Marcuse's terms, repressive and de-sublimating, as fascinating and repulsive, as de-alienation on one level and re-alienating on another: the highly ambivalent formation of a blocked crisis.[3] In other words we have been seduced into managing our own alienation, but in a world in which the division between good and evil has been relocated in the general process of secularization and disenchantment: yet it is right in front of us.

There is from this point an intensification of the poetic within Baudrillard's prose writing itself. Up to the publication of *L'Ange de Stuc* (1978), Baudrillard held a number of structures apart: prose, poetry, and his mode of living in the world. As he has reported in an important interview (1983d), from about the writing of *Seduction* (1979), but certainly since 1980, he has attempted to suture these particular formal separations. This is certainly evident in the difference between the highly referenced social science framework of *Symbolic Exchange and Death* (1976) and the later texts which are without formal references rely more fundamentally on examples and cases drawn from literature and from his own life,[4] and presented in aphorism (*Cool Memories* vols 1 and 2, 1987b).

Nevertheless there is still a strong theoretical reference framework in the structure of genealogies already established in the works up to 1976, and the apparently dominant form is that of the analytic and the semiological, since these works attempt in the first place to produce arguments in theory. However, as will become clear, Baudrillard is far from content to remain in a conventional communicative mode, arguing within the frame of a rational system of references, developing his ideas as part of a project.

What is interesting here is his attempt to jump out of this framework: it is lived as a form of death. His basic problem is that the rational or scientific determinations of our action have a strictly narrow sphere, if they truly operate at all. What exists beyond them? It is clear that Baudrillard lived this line of thought himself: his answers to these questions may not, as yet, be fully convincing, but they are undeniably remarkable.

But what is certain at this point is that a fundamental transformation has taken place. This is plain in the first sentence of *Fatal Strategies*, which begins: 'Things have found a way to escape the dialectic of meaning' (Baudrillard 1983b: 9). Baudrillard himself follows a course away from the 'dialectic' conceived in the narrow sense (that is, restricted to the movement of historical meaning). Baudrillard here approaches via another mode of thought, one directly exemplified by Canetti, who is cited approvingly:

> A tormenting thought: as of a certain point, history was no longer real. Without noticing it, all mankind suddenly left reality; everything which happened since then was supposedly not true; but we supposedly didn't notice. Our task would now be to find that point, as long as we didn't have it, we would be forced to abide in our present destruction.
>
> (Canetti 1978: 69, cited in Baudrillard 1983b: 18)

Later, talking about this perspective in an interview (in 1987c: 67–8), Baudrillard explained:

> this idea appeals to me because Canetti doesn't envisage an end, but rather what I would call an 'ecstasy', in the primal sense of the word – a passage at the same time into the dissolution and the transcendence of a form.

In *Fatal Strategies* he refers to the concept of

> the dead point where every system passes through the subtle limit of reversibility, of contradiction and re-evaluation, in order to be completely absorbed in non-contradiction, in desperate self-contemplation and in ecstasy.
>
> (1988b: 190)

But, Baudrillard argues, if it is the case, as Canetti believes, that it is possible to retrace steps and find this point where 'history is no longer real' (in fact it is said to be 'our task'), by what miracle could one return to the real or the true? It was the point at which linear time ended. And perhaps it came to a definitive end. In this case after a certain point it is impossible to recapture the past. It as if humanity violated a secret law, or committed a fatal imprudence. It is useless, he says in a rather forced provocation to theory, to ask these questions, just as it is to ask why a woman leaves you: this is mysterious and nothing can be changed in any case, a statement indicative of the new fatalistic mood (1983b: 20).[5] After a certain point all efforts to exorcize the past serve nothing, for it is in the end naive to think that events follow and obey human wishes. Canetti's view, then, is pious, even if his hypothesis is a radical one. It is impossible to find the dead point, even if this point has ever existed. Nevertheless others have sought to find a way back, to try to re-enter history, time, reality, the social, 'as a satellite lost in hyperspace returns to earth', but this is a false radicalism.

However, beyond the dead point there are only events without consequences and theories. Events presage nothing, for beyond them lies only catastrophe. Everything, including language, finds its own mode of disappearance. The disconnection is complete: like the man without qualities, the body without organs, as time without memory: now it becomes event without consequence. And if this is the case, all interpretations are possible, and we arrive at the position of the equi-probability of all interpretation and theory, and all theories can convert into each other.

As if to delight in the malicious implication of this, Baudrillard's essay itself converts into a prose poem as he begins to evoke the referential illusion that abolishes all referents, the slowing down of things as they reach a catastrophic point. It is, he says, no longer the devouring fire in the sky which strikes us. Not the deluge, the maternal deluge of the origin of the world. Nor even the nuclear explosion, or the big bang of the origin of the universe. Now it is the earthquake as if the earth never really existed, was only a skin without depth. The new situation entails a requiem for infrastructures as we fear falling into the void.

Ironically any state of power which could foresee the earthquake would be more in danger than those who suffer from the earthquake itself. Witness the action of the *terremotati* who have violently attacked the Italian state and its system of security, its mass media, as having been responsible for the destructiveness of the earthquake it attempted to deal with, 'justifiably', says Baudrillard. It is the same in relation to terrorism, for counter-terrorist measures inflict more damage than terrorists: and in order to eradicate terrorism a totally terroristic system would have to be installed. The catastrophe.

Pompeii is the site of the catastrophe and indeed a second one, a recent earthquake.[6] What is essential at Pompeii, he suggests, is not monumentality nor beauty, but the 'fatal intimacy of things', 'and the fascination in their instantaneity as a perfect simulacrum of our own death' (1983b: 31). He evokes the mental effect of catastrophe, to apprehend things before they reach their end, in a state of ghostly suspension.

Pompeii. Everything is metaphysical, a double simulation: the freezing of time is mirrored by the heat of the day, the geometry is a mental geometry of labyrinths. The conjunction of the banality of strolling through them in the immanence of another time, the unique moment of catastrophe. Reflection: the deadly presence of Vesuvius gives the charm of hallucination to these dead roads. The illusion: of being here and now at this place on the eve of the eruption and resurrection two thousand years later by a miracle of nostalgia. Strangeness. No history is interposed between these things 'in the heat where death seized them' and us. Pompeii is thus a *trompe-l'oeil* and primitive scene: vertigo (without time) and hallucination (but with complete transparency of detail). The second catastrophe is like the sadistic irony of fate which is drawn as it were to destroy this beauty. Yet it plays with the place by turning it into a second eternity. A 'blasting (*sideration*) of a teeming presence of life in a catastrophic instant' (1983b: 32).[7] Pompeii has suffered its last event or act produced by nature itself under the guise of parody (1983b: 33).

This scene of the Pompeii ruins introduces the transpolitical, a term developed specifically to evoke the

> transparency and obscenity of all the structures of a destructured universe, the transparency and obscenity of change in a universe without history . . . end of the scene of history, end of the scene of phantasy, end of the scene of the body – irruption of the obscene. End of the secret – irruption of transparency.
>
> (1983b: 37)

This is no longer of mode of production. That which is passionate now is a mode of disappearance. The horizon of meaning is at an end. Now the question concerns the saturation (obesity) of systems of memory, of information, the escalation into excess (*excroissance*), even thinkable as a new metastatic cancerous equilibrium:

an ecstatic state of crisis. The basic nature of transpolitical forms, and their enigma, can be seen in the shift from the secret to the transparent, from the scene to the obscene (the enigma reduced to a puzzle). This is a new era which marks the movement from the violent world of transgression and anomie to that where basic forms escape the norm, and, as error, lead to the event without consequence (the earthquake: parody of an irruption).

OBESITY

One important transpolitical form is that of obesity, characteristic of western societies and affluent cultures. It is an obscene form related not just to abundance, but to significant modifications of food and taste. For Baudrillard, this is marked in the transition to a regressive orality, the improvement of food by a glamour system which matches that of the cinema and film. In theory, these gross forms come into existence when cultural and physical controls lose their effectiveness. The result is the bloated figure, the figure of Jarry's pataphysical Ubu, but now entered into reality itself. This, however, is only one side of a vast cultural shift which reveals itself in the displacement of oppressed groups by disabled groups. Against the contradictions formed in the previous period, all such polarities are displaced by a pataphysical substitution: the mentally and physically disabled are now thrown against the system (1983b: 43). The social system begins to develop programmes out of its own 'living waste' in search of new bases of legitimacy. Here the management of monstrosity replaces earlier forms of crisis management. Mockingly, Baudrillard describes the attempts to help the disabled as new self-defeating mechanisms which further clog the system: rails for the blind block the routes for wheelchairs. (Every time Baudrillard comes across the disabled he finds some basis for a joke: at whose expense? No doubt the system, but also curiously, as if a cruel world demanded it, of the disabled themselves. Now the revolutionary slogan must be, he concludes: to each according to his deficiency.)

The contemporary form of the revolt, he argues, is that of the body against itself, cancerous and metastatic phenomena at the genetic level. Here there is, potentially, undisciplined proliferation, an instability which cannot be maintained. These cancerous formations have overambition, a kind of hypertelia, appearing to offer affinities with the nature of the hyperreal itself: it revolts against the genetic order, as if it were disobeying a law. The body seems to revolt against its own internal regime, disturbs its own balance, in a form which is, he remarks, none the less, mysteriously esoteric. Obesity is an ascent to extremes in a field where the rule has been withdrawn. For theory the decisive point is that its logic is that of a realization of potential, an excess of potential, on a single plane: potentialization, not dialectical progression. There are no longer structures of distinctive opposition, no contrastive field.

TERRORISM

A second transpolitical form is that of terrorism and the hostage, which seems to have an 'affinity' with the mass (now no longer a reference point for meaning, no longer a sociological reality, simply a 'shadow cast by power' (1983a: 48)). However serious claims are that there is some representation here, terrorism is always divorced from the mass, but to the hyperreality of the masses (they do not exist as a reality) terrorism replies with 'an equally hyperreal act'. The aim of the terrorist, he suggests, is a kind of

> mental downgrading by contingency, fascination and panic, not to a reflection or to the logic of cause and effect, but to a chain reaction by contagion – senseless and indeterminate like the system it combats.
>
> (1983a: 51)

Clearly, he says, terrorism does not aim at influencing opinion polls or at mobilizing public opinion. It is not revolutionary. It is consistent with the very silence of the masses. Its aim seems to be to attempt to destroy the 'white magic of the social' in order to immediately precipitate its death. Such violence appears indeterminate, senseless, and blind. Terrorism and the masses 'are the most radical, most intense contemporary form of the denial of the whole representative system' (1983a: 52). And this raises an acute problem for analysis for

> noone really knows what relation can be established between two elements that are outside representation, this is a problem to which our epistemology of knowledge permits no resolution.
>
> (1983a: 52)

This, for Baudrillard then, is an uncharted terrain, where the only links are 'analogical, affinitive'. He speculates that there may be an exchange of energy of a completely different kind from that of accumulation, one of 'social dispersal, of dispersal of the social, of absorption and anulment' (1983a: 53).

The dominant feature of terrorism, and its specific character, is that it does not aim at the unmasking of the state. It implies the non-representational character of power, and it is in this feature that its subversiveness is to be found. All the major institutions of representation are thus threatened by it, albeit in small but powerful doses. When modern terrorists take hostages it is often the case that there does not appear to be a direct enemy, the enemy is purely mythical and undifferentiated. The blindness of terror is a replica of the system's own undifferentiated nature. In fact, in the sense that anyone could be a hostage, it can be imagined that everyone is always predestined to be one (1983a: 53).

The terrorist act is therefore something like a natural catastrophe, and the terrorist is a 'mythological equivalent' of the imminent social catastrophe.

Terrorism as a transpolitical form is the 'more than violent' political excess. A certain threshold has been crossed, a set of rules has been withdrawn. But the basic significance of the taking of hostages is reflected in the reaction and implications it inevitably involves. Society is thrown into a new search for security,[8] but it is the 'fractal zone' which is the specific space for the terrorist: the no-man's land of international airports, embassies. It is from these 'extraterrestrial' spaces that hostages are taken, and this mirrors the very ecstatic form of violence that terrorism develops and is again mirrored in the state's response. This escalates into ecstasy as the masses tend to indifference. This is because in most cases the terrorist does not represent anything, and nor does the hostage: a frozen, obscene form of disappearance. Take, as example, the kidnapping of Aldo Morro in Italy by the Red Brigades, who eventually killed him and threw his body at the feet of the Communist Party. This, says Baudrillard, reveals the exhibitionist nature of terrorism, and its affinity with the media as another form of the obscenity of information: without the media, no terrorism. Essentially the problem here, argues Baudrillard, is that exchange comes to an end, and as terrorism moves to the limit in the abolition of exchange it reveals the fact that it is exchange which protects us from the fatal and from destiny. For that which cannot be exchanged becomes a pure object, that is, at one and the same time very precious, but one which cannot be let go or passed to another, cannot be negotiated away.[9] If it is dangerous it will be killed, and then the cadaver itself will take its revenge. Cancelled as object the hostage is still dangerous in a form very much like the talisman or the fetish. The problem of exchange for the terrorist is, however, still secondary, for terrorism is utopian and projects itself outside of exchange by means of the escalation of the challenge in the duel. A banal situation is made into a transpolitical figure.

OBSCENITY

A third such figure is that of the obscene. In all western culture this is realized in the historical loss of the secret, poetic, theatrical, the loss of illusion. A new sovereignty arises in relation to appearance, whereas for the secret there is only an inner complicity. The difficulties in the west follow on strictly from the collapse of illusion, the collapse therefore into an obscenity, the real beyond all redeeming artifice. These cultures, become terroristic themselves, are still vulnerable to the forces of seduction, and must at some level find a response to the challenge, and indeed must at some level also find a challenge to the real (1983b: 72). Fundamentally the illusion is not to be equated with the idea of the false, for it is quite different to understand it as that which enchants, that which is more subtle than the real. It is necessary to work at the strategic level of the second degree, that which is more false than false as a challenge to the real itself (for example in the *trompe-l'oeil*). The real, reality, must be humiliated, just as it has humiliated illusion, for only in this way can obscenity itself be unhinged.

THE LOGIC OF ESCALATION

It is when the object escalates to the extremes, says Baudrillard, that things proceed to a strange logic of inverse effects. As in seduction, where a form of the more false than false evolves, the effect seems to attain all the power and the splendour of the true. Like a great work of art, it glows with the power of a reversal of energy. The good is alive and glows with the energy of evil. There is a decisive transpositioning of energy from pole to pole, so that appearances are both subverted and redoubled. At this extreme obscenity can burst into the transparent world, but not, as Bataille for instance thought, as a genuinely transgressive force (perhaps the idea is the last hope of political economy), but as subtle inversion and potentialization.

In this escalation of effects to extremes Baudrillard begins to consider, not a set of constraints, but a simultaneous logic of doublings and inversions of energies, to grasp the opposed radical effects of obscenity and seduction as they interweave themselves. Take gambling, for example. What happens to money here can never fully be achieved in a passive theory (as in Brenner 1990) or even in sophisticated statistical theories of probability suitably turned towards the mystical (Stewart 1990). In effect what occurs is not the production or destruction of money, but rather here money is made to disappear as value only to resurface as appearance, and in such a pure form that an immediate reversibility is possible. In this form money is naked and in free circulation in a strictly formal sense: it is a cold, superficial passion, and totally obscene in structure. In effect money has ceased to exist. This game ascends to the plane of the disappearance of all power as with all such forms of white magic. Money disappears as value and as essence, he says in another theoretical provocation, in the escalation without limit. The particular benefits of this mode of theorizing now begin to appear and justify themselves in new concepts and a new epistemology that does not base itself in a framework of system or of countervailing forces.

Ironically, Baudrillard says, it is with the destruction of such secrets, the secret of money in gambling, that our condition becomes fatal. But this fatality is of a special type suited to our particular ecstasy. Our ecstasy is a phenomenon of the loss of a particular world, which contained the secret, and of the recovery of a world in a kind of 'spectral lubricity' which covers our institutions and idols, the melancholy index that these institutions and idols have already begun to die. This is to be explained by the simple fact that there is never such obscenity when the social is in the social, or the sexual is in sex. As society has lost its basic determinations, it becomes funereal, society is haunted by the loss of the social, just as at the level of the individual there is an anxiety at the loss of sexual authenticity (1983b: 78). In this process of the loss of structures and distinctions, each social instance loses the specifity and nature it established in a previous period (now paradoxically celebrated by Baudrillard and taken as the measure of transfinite phenomena). The sexual begins to invade every sphere, but then itself disappears in its distinctiveness. When everything becomes indiscriminately political, or cultural, this marks the end for the specifically political and cultural, and transpolitical figures emerge across the face of society.

In this respect, in a certain triumphant return to his predictions in his earlier writings, it can now be seen just how mistaken was the idea that an instance like sex could be made into a subversive principle in order to unravel enigmas in all other spheres. This conceptualization raises immediate problems for Baudrillard's own fusional (transtheoretical) writings. But here he avoids reflection. This could only lead to a general precipitation into indifferentiation, into an analytic fog where all maladies become simply psychosomatic. What really happens is the devaluation of a category, and the emergence of analytic common denominators, as in any multidisciplinary project where the different sides pass on their lowest order concepts to each other. The result is a general anaesthetization. The loss is never compensated. It is in this way, he suggests, that the world moves from a Promethean and Faustian stage of production and consumption, to that of interfaces, contact, feedback, connection, and network (1983b: 92). Baudrillard here notes the obverse of the other form of catastrophe, the ecstatic aestheticization.

In this new world of the perfection of objects in their very abstraction and functionality the keyboard and the console occupy a new space, one which begins also to homogenize all the elements around them. Such a process of perfection of objects, at all levels but particularly at the level of miniaturization, makes the human body or the countryside appear utterly useless and imperfect, and the drama of alienation with its romantic aesthetic passes to the ecstasy of communication (1983b: 93). It is important, he says, only to note that the drama of the spectacle was never obscene, for this begins only from the moment that there is no more scene, that is, where everything is transparent. Clearly consumer society still maintained something of a veil over its internal processes, even though, as Marx recognized, the structure of the commodity had already become obscene. In order to understand what has happened it is only necessary, he insists, in following a technique which will inevitably produce a vision of a homogeneous universe (something in fact Marx himself very consciously avoided doing), to follow and extend Marx's analysis to the domains now touched by the same process to arrive at a theory of the universe of pure communication:

It isn't only the sexual which has become obscene in pornography, today there is also a pornography of information and communication, circuits and networks, a pornography of functions, of objects in their readability, their fluidity, their availability, their regulation, their polyvalency, their forced signification, in their free expression. Obscenity is wholly soluble in communication.

(1983b: 94)

There is an important modification of the forms of involvement in these processes, best described, Baudrillard argues, as a move from hot or black obscenity, to cool, white obscenity. Baudrillard intensifies the images again, this time adopting a sociological genealogy of the game, as examined in the work of Caillois (Caillois 1962). He suggests that games have evolved from expressive rituals, from competitive games to games of chance and vertigo. In these latter games there is a change of form to that of personal, solitary games where the dominant engagement is cool, narcissicistic, where pleasure is close to becoming psychotropic in cool fascination. At the points where these become totally absorbing the forms approach a dimension of schizophrenia: the player and the world lose their specificities, the environment itself begins to exceed its boundaries, the self loses its boundaries and enters into the obscenity of things, events lose their distinctiveness in time in an over-exposure of the interiority of the world to itself (1983b: 97). But there is another sense of forcing to extremes again here as Baudrillard adds more of the same to evoke an overwhelming general tendency. He seems to sense this.

There are, in looking at the emergence of these transpolitical objects, two possible judgements that can be made, he maintains. One is that nothing has really changed and that we are still at the stage where a revolutionary transcendence will eliminate them in a new historical progressive liberation, a utopia is still possible. Or, that this stage has already been reached and these phenomena belong to the utopia. The utopia that this may be, he posits, is thus already beyond the end of things, and all metaphors have 'penetrated reality'. This is a transfinite universe, and it is our destiny. The evocation of the catastrophe has been achieved as a mirror image of the Renaissance reading of the symbolic: a lurid ecstasy.

Driven relentlessly to explore these problems he again reordered, in 1990, his forms of exposition to be able to discuss the transaesthetic, the transsexual, and the transeconomic. Now they reflected a more sombre mood and the writing becomes cooler, polished. The mania for extremes passes into a subdued obsession.

TRANSAESTHETIC OBJECTS

Baudrillard's discussion directly picks up his ideas on art established in his earliest writings; modern art can be characterized as having broken its pact with the symbolic order (1990b: 22). Today it is completely dominated by the proliferation of signs, by the massive recycling of forms, past and present. There no longer exists any rule, any criterion for judgement or taste, indeed any pleasure. The game has become entirely formal, like a game of floating money and utter individualism, where currencies cannot be converted into goods. It is the end of hidden orders, and allusive complicities, which gave culture its force. Now there is only a total indifference of new fashions, new geometricism, new abstractionism, new figurationism. . . . This form of overbidding only induces new proliferations into disorder which breaks the code of the aesthetic sphere itself, just as the genetic code is broken by biological disorder.

But this art broadens out and spreads across all social spheres in its incessant mixing of styles and anti-styles, cultural and anti-cultural in its effects in one single general aesthetic. From Duchamp to Warhol all objects have to be liberated, all the insignificant things in the world are transfigured into the aesthetic. The ironic single gain of the Campbell soup tin is that we no longer have to endure the monotony of discussion of the beautiful and the ugly which dominated former discourse, for here all the previous analytic distinctions fall away. In their place is stupefaction in the face of a continuous stream of images, videos, plastic objects which pass without leaving a trace, shadow, or consequence. The single monochrome painting is marvellously abstract in its geometrical nullity, having effaced all aesthetic syntax: the transaesthetic object.

This effacement, however, like the Byzantine icons which never permit the questioning of the existence of God, presents a reality or hyperreality that exists without permitting a question to arise. These objects are transparent, and it is useless to begin a search for meaning, just as we would never dream, he says, of searching in the infra-red or ultra-violet for the colour of the sky (Baudrillard 1990b: 26). These works are indeed transaesthetic in the sense that they begin to occupy a space beyond the beautiful and the ugly. The logic of their evolution is quite different, it is more ugly than ugly, ugliness taken to a second degree. Liberated from the real it is necessary to escalate to the second degree: the hyperreal. It was with hyperrealism in art, and pop art, that the powers of the everyday became elevated to the ironic level of photorealism, a mode which today dominates and envelops all art. This state of ecstasy is mirrored in the art market where the logic is found in the movement from the dear to the more dear than dear, a gambling logic of outbidding which takes off into its own pataphysical solution.

THE TRANSSEXUAL

For Baudrillard, it is clear that the body is destined for a curious, artificial future, a mode of transsexuality dominated by a mode of transvestism, the play of signs across the sexes as a challenge to the very structure of sexual difference. But, whether it is surgical or semiurgical, it is, he suggests, still a matter of artificial organs or limbs, of prostheses: the destiny of the body itself in the new environment is itself to become an artificial organ, a prosthesis. But we are all on the way to becoming transsexual. Our images move in this direction. Take, for example, Cicciolina the Italian pornography star: she has the classic form of the innocence of pornography, a glacial aesthetic, devoid of all charm, even all sensuality; she is a well-muscled android, synthetic, a kind of 'carnal ectoplasm' who belongs to the same universe as the androgynous Frankenstein, Michael Jackson. These are mutants, genetically baroque gender benders, their erotic appeal scarcely veils a sexual indetermination.

Michael Jackson is rather like Andy Warhol, as he attains a state which is perfectly artificial, innocent and pure, androgynous, a machine. Warhol said that all his works of art are beautiful, art is everywhere, and it does not exist any more. The modern aesthetic is radically agnostic. This is mirrored in transsexual kitsch. The myth of the sexual revolution can be found here, but not in the conventional form. In the period of the orgy, sexual liberation, sexuality still functioned on the basis of sexual difference. This period has passed, and today it is the transvestite form which dominates, which tends to merge together all the erotic themes and signs into a postmodern pornography where sexuality begins to lose itself in ambiguity and theatrical excess. Sexuality no longer retains its radical and subversive charge. Cicciolina can even be elected to the Italian parliament and the transsexual and the transpolitical political meet.

It is interesting to note (again implicitly raising reflexive problems for himself) that even fashion moves to the second degree in the period dominated by transvestism, as everyone is induced not to be in fashion but to adopt an individual 'look'. This makes fashion a performance, as everyone searches for an act of appearance, rather, he says, indicating the timelessness of his own problematic, as if McLuhan's notion of the tactile image has been generalized beyond its immediate domain into a field of differential play without any particular conviction, and so fashion becomes a disenchanted form after all, an indifferent, transient mannerism. This indeed casts, he suggests, a curious light on the sexual revolution once thought to be an irruption of maximal erotic value, the rise to privilege of the feminine and of pleasure. In fact, in retrospect, this phase was simply a short episode on the way to the confusion of genders, of transsexualism. But, he notes, this may well be the fate of all revolutions since it appears that one of the fundamental revolutions, that of technique ends in the same way: am I person or machine? We have become transsexual in the way we have become transpolitical in general: undifferentiated and indifferent.

TRANSECONOMIC PHENOMENA

The Crash of 1987: was it a crash? It was and it was not, this is the problem of the new transeconomic object. And here Baudrillard's analysis suddenly produces something completely unexpected, a position which brings him back into touch with critical theory.[10] The only adequate way to think about this issue now, he argues, is to think of the catastrophe as virtual, which means, he notes, that there will be no crash, a conclusion which he uses to reorganize once again many of his basic assumptions. The reason for the absence of the crash is that there has developed a surprising separation between what he calls the fictional and the real economy. This is strictly parallel to the separation between conventional and nuclear war; and the separation works to the benefit of all since the separation has the important effect of making war impossible. What is necessary is to register this fact theoretically, the virtual catastrophe renders the real catastrophe obsolete.

This means that the new form of capital which has come into

existence exists, as it were, in orbit. In strict contrast with the situation in the 1920s, a crash now does not entail a slump in the economy as a whole; it appears that the real economy can absorb it. To the immense embarrassment of all theory, capitalism has become virtual capitalism.[11] Marx thought that capital would stumble from crisis to crisis, crash to crash, but, like nuclear war, this did not happen.

What did occur has to be understood as a transeconomic effect, as a hyperrealization of finance capital, which orbiting in the stratosphere like nuclear weaponry escapes the necessary connections of reality itself. Economies continue to produce, although logically the immense fluctuations in capital movement should cause a fundamental inhibition. The same is true of the important issue of the world debt. Should the economies be forced to face up to the strict economic consequences of this debt all exchange would stop immediately. But

> when a debt is launched into space, it begins to circulate from one bank to another, from one country to another, it actually redeems itself – and that is how we finish – by forgetting, by putting into an endless orbital circulation all the atomic detritus and all other forms of waste.
>
> (Baudrillard 1989d: 66)

So the dream of a reconciliation of real and the fictional economies will never be realized. The 'money' in the fictional economy is simply not convertible into the real one. This is a happy outcome since, should it be possible, the immediate result would be world catastrophic collapse. This may appear, as it does with the nuclear threat, as a monstrous eccentricity, but it is surely, he argues, our best hope. World overpopulation, world debt, nuclear war, economic crash can therefore become acceptable to us, as virtual bombs, which if left 'in their excess, in their sheer hyper-reality [keep] the world intact' (1989d: 66). He writes as if this were a provocation to others, yet it is surely a decisive challenge to his whole framework. But he continues to focus on the hyperreal, not as yet concerned to investigate the new separation he has introduced.

Marxism once dreamed of the extinction of classes and political economy in a world in which the social would become transparent. But now political economy has moved in a different direction, one which is radical and unforeseen. It has begun to disappear 'by its own self mutation into a speculative transeconomy . . . a pure game of floating and arbitrary rules, a fatal game of catastrophe' (1989d: 67). Thus the very term 'economy' begins to alter its sense. It is no longer motor, productive infrastructure. It is the sphere of the process of the destructuration of value. The era is one of pure speculation, the emergence of an 'economy' cleared of all 'real' economic effects, a viral economy which has to align itself with all the other viral processes (1990b: 41).

Yet something has happened. It might be called, in line with Baudrillard's concerns, an inconspicuous mode of the reappearance of the real. Half acknowledged, it is *a reversal of his conceptualization of the evolution of capitalism*. This is surprisingly confirmed in his concern to move to analyses of a different style, of cultural objects once more, either of buildings (the Beaubourg) or astonishingly of whole cultures: America as Object. Here we see *the emergence of new analytic styles which begin to identify complex objects*. In these analyses evocation, aphorism, poetry, description combine to evolve a concrete analysis of astonishing critical power.

From the Beaubourg to the Bonaventure Hotel

is this postmodernism?
Baudrillard

THE BEAUBOURG EFFECT

The Beaubourg Effect is Baudrillard's critique of the high-modernist Pompidou Centre in Paris. Written after *Symbolic Exchange*, it none the less employs all its new theoretical means in an essay of devastating power. The essay has been influential: it has been used by Fredric Jameson as a resource to elaborate a general characterization of the present mode of western culture as post-modern, a form of culture generated by late capitalism. But at the time of writing this essay the term postmodernism had not become current, and in any case it is unlikely that Baudrillard would have used it, for Baudrillard's basic orientations are in another direction (and the essay has to be understood and read in the context of the theory emerging in the mid-1970s to which this essay belongs). The essay, though only brief, was published as a book in 1977 (it also appears in 1981a: 93–111, and in English translation, 1982). In this chapter the main lines of its arguments are presented and then its poetic structure examined in detail.

The main outline of the essay is as follows. The Pompidou Centre, the 'Beaubourg', is notable for displaying its pipes and ducts on the outside of the building, a facade of networks and circuits. But, in essence, says Baudrillard, the building has all the culturally deterrent power of the black monolith out of the film *2001*. It may appear explosive, but in effect, it is implosive, as it absorbs energy from its environment and impoverishes it by estab-lishing something of its own security zone around itself, rather like a nuclear power station. But the technology of circulation which is all too evident works less well when it comes to people. Inside there is modern space, modern ambience, and people adopt a suitably cool comportment. But paradoxically the Beaubourg attempts to maintain something of the old culture, which gives the impression that the whole building seems to have been constructed without any genuine awareness of its role and function, for this is a monument to polyvalency, total visibility, and security values which are completely opposed to culture.

The interior culture gives the impression not of living vital art, but of a certain form of reanimation, since all the contents are anachronistic. It is a fitting monument only to cultural disconnection, to hyperreality, a culture that is transient and recyclable (it reassembles units or particles which are all the same). The emphasis on production and the factory, or refinery, means that the centre aligns itself against the more fundamental elements of initiation, secret, and ritual. There is a real problem of what to put in this building, what to exhibit, since the whole building signifies the disappearance of meaning: the interior appeals to the culture in depth of an earlier period, it is sustained by this reference. But, today, the separation between the signifier and the signified has disappeared, and truth is empty. The Beaubourg should be a hyperreal labyrinth, not a factory, a labyrinth of division, fascination, simulation, and implosion.

But in effect the Beaubourg brings an immense transmutation of traditional culture towards a type of homogeneity, just like the façade and its pipework. The building is thus part of anti-culture, and the irony is that the masses are summoned to it in the name of culture and when they arrive they find a version of the third order of simulation: the hyperreal. Even so the masses detested high culture and they have come as if to a natural catastrophe. Ironically again, their very weight threatens the monument. This must be interpreted as a strategy, as the strategy that the masses themselves adopt in order to bring mass culture itself to an end.

The real content of the Beaubourg then is probably the mass itself. It is its raw material, and the building could easily be taken as a giant refinery. Yet the mass is formed only by a question posed by the centre, by the object, which is more like a super- or hypermarket than it is a museum. It is a simulation of the homogenous space–time of society itself and like a hypermarket it has no memory (unlike a traditional museum), only stock. In this sense the true output of the Beaubourg is not art or culture at all, it is only a form of the mass and mass anti-culture. The violence of the object stock is transferred to the mass: above 30,000 people and the building is in danger of collapse. The mass aims 'expressly and knowingly' for this abolition, it challenges a sterile culture with physical annihilation. This response is, above all, tactile. For the world is no longer that of representation, reflection, of critical distance. It is no longer that of critical discourse and debate, or figure. It is world of touch and manipulation, and in the Beaubourg people want to 'accept everything, swipe everything, eat everything, touch everything. . . . The organisers are alarmed by this uncontrollable impulse.'

What this brings into being is a form of panic in slow motion, an implosive violence that exists only as a mode of disappearance. Up to this period everyone is habituated to thinking in terms of dialectical expansion, displacement, and transcendence. Today violence is different. The system no longer expands, it is saturated and begins to contract. Violence now becomes a sequence of increasing density, of network overload. This is a process which is no longer indeterminate and random and defies our notion of causality. Thus an image such as Bataille's notion of the sun as provider of light as sumptuary expenditure has to be reconsidered: this sun today is in a condition of terminal implosion en route to the black hole. Indeed May '68 in France was the first implosive episode, a reaction against saturation, an involution. Subsequently, radio piracy has developed (mainly in Italy) which reveals a new order of implosive revolution which defies the universal, which is subverted from increasingly dense and ungraspable points.[1]

That is the general argument of the essay in brief outline, and is sufficient to suggest that it forms a complex web of metaphors, indeed what might well be called the 'Baudrillard effect'.[2] But precisely what kind of text is this: art criticism, sociology, poetry, literature? Although rigorous, the essay represents an enormous compression, evidently a compression of the theory developed at great length in *L'Echange Symbolique et La Mort*, published a year ealier, but it also represents an enormous change of style from that essay, which was the last of Baudrillard's works to conform to an academic, fully referenced form of working. In *The Beaubourg Effect*, the style is polemical, fast, direct, concise, yet it rests on the fundamental ground of the problematic of the object.

INITIAL READING

A first reading might interpret the essay in the following way: the Beaubourg is an object which destroys the difference between surface and interior; it fetishizes circulation (fluids, masses, money). It installs the ambience of the modern interior on all surfaces in functionality and polyvalency. The world takes on the shape of the moebius ring, which, in twisting back on itself, annihilates the difference between the outside and the inside. And this is mirrored in the objects of contemporary culture, which are superficial and pure simulation.

But the Beaubourg is also productive of the mass; as ironic outcome of its anti-cultural process, the mass arrives for the spectacle of the funeral of culture and of mass culture: it arrives for sacrilege. The organizers, the police, the intellectuals, and the building itself, however, create a security zone of high surveillance, but around a function which is antiquated. The interior tries to devote itself to eternal values, but the building is devoted to transience and obsolescence. The irony is that the Beaubourg tries to promote a culture, but actually is dissuasive: it should at least have tried to have evoked a suitable culture of contemporary simulation. But cultural and political criticism cannot now bring down the Beaubourg, since polyvalent culture can absorb all opposition into its system of differences. The Beaubourg can still be brought down physically, through the weight of the mass.[3] Beyond the Beaubourg there is the possibility of an implosive resistance at particular sites which escape the general logic.

This interpretation immediately poses the question of Baudrillard's relation to such an object and such a culture: is he himself drawn into the black hole? Obviously he regards himself as privileged here. For he knows what culture is, and he talks on its behalf. He also locates strategies of opposition in the masses with which he associates himself, and even, sarcastically, formulates some slogans, like 'Make it Fold'. There is, however, an attraction–repulsion, since his own strategy appears to reveal and expose ironic contradictions in the functioning of the building, and to explain these on the basis of his theory of the difference between symbolic exchange and simulation.

TOWARDS AN ANALYSIS OF COMPLEX CULTURAL OBJECTS

What is striking is the complexity and density of the writing. The essay begins with the crucial question: what can he call the Beaubourg? – Effect, Machine, Thing?

> The enigma of this carcass of signs and of flux, of networks and circuits – the ultimate velleity of the translation of an unnameable structure: that of social relations consigned to a superficial ventilation (animation, self management, information, media) and to an irreversible implosion in depth.
>
> (Baudrillard 1981a: 93)

It does not have a name; it does not have its concept. He toys with the idea of 'machine', 'thing', 'effect'. He calls his essay 'The Beaubourg Effect', yet in the essay it is also called an object, and in a sense the question is: is this object part of the object system? It certainly may be, but what Baudrillard has signalled here is a shift in conception of the object away from the passive, ordering, classifying modality of his first works, to the vision of object as active, as challenge, as effect. But the complexity is evident in the first lines of the essay: how to conceive of the complexity of the combination of the two sides of the equation already doubled up (A, i and ii; B, i and ii):

A. i) carcass   death, rotting body
    ii) signs, flux   life, communication
B. i) surface/ventilation   pipes, tubes, heat
       superficial/ventilation $\left\{\begin{array}{l}\text{information networks,}\\\text{circulation, media}\end{array}\right.$

    ii) irreversible
        implosion in depth   death

He congratulates the planners for having provided an irony of modern culture: it aims to educate but does the reverse. He attacks the socialists for thinking they can criticize the building for not taking into account the cultural aspirations of the masses.

But he is quite prepared to say what should be exhibited in such a building, that which is equal to it, or indeed would challenge it at its own level:

> it should be a labyrinth, a library of infinite permutations, an aleatory redistribution of destinies by the game or lottery – in

brief the Borgesian universe – or yet Circular Ruins . . . an experiment in all the different processes of representation: diffraction, implosion . . . chance connections and disconnections – in short a culture of simulation and fascination.

(1981a: 99)

There is inherently a possible form of play here, Baudrillard suggests, a play within a certain seductive structure of simulation. Yet the contemporary culture is out of synchrony, and hinged back on to the past and the culture of meaning, or into unseductive simulation.

These possibilities are inherent as affinities, and it is important to examine the affinities more widely. The most obvious affinity is that of the social mass with the physical mass of objects and raw materials which pass through the building. The images also build up here: the mass of stock, the mass of objects without purpose, the mass integrated by the magnetism of particles, and the critical mass, the critical weight which will bring the building down. In commerce the mass is seduced by the attraction of the crowd, and because this mass is inside the building further mass will be attracted inside, a kind of auto-agglutination of the mass which can only accelerate in a chain reaction. These affinities are doubled into those around the image of violence: that of the collapse of the building is mirrored in the violence of stocking itself, the violence of the implosive process, the violence of a panic in slow motion, the destruction of cities not by a fire but by saturation, as of networks by overload, and the violence of cultural dissuasion. The problem, he suggests, is that this object is unprecedented and is unimaginable, indecipherable, as it leaves all previous epistemologies in suspension (since they are founded on the universe in expansion). Baudrillard's language here is that of saturation, densification, overload, overregulation, implosion.

The image of implosion is therefore central: star systems, he notes, do not end simply when their radiational level has been expended. They slow down and their collapse accelerates, they become involuted and their energy can no longer escape to the outside. They become black holes after a final fabulous burst of energy. This image of the black hole is obviously only part of the net of nuclear metaphors which seem to build up in the following way:

BEAUBOURG
is:

1. a black monolith $\left\{\begin{array}{l}\text{a mix of images which} \\ \text{suggest both fission,} \\ \text{danger, collapse}\end{array}\right.$
   black box
   nuclear station
   black hole
   an incinerator

2. a circulating fluid $\left\{\begin{array}{l}\text{decomposition,} \\ \text{recycling,} \\ \text{recombination} \\ \text{transparency}\end{array}\right.$
   mass in circulation
   oil refinery
   circulating current
   network of circuits
   surface flux

3. a crushed car $\left\{\begin{array}{l}\text{death,} \\ \text{compression}\end{array}\right.$
   carcass

There are two different processes at work here, one of fission, of breaking into parts, fragments; the other is one of fusion, of attraction and combination. It is around the mass that the ideas of fusion gravitate: the mass in circulation, in panic, the mass in overload, in saturation. Fusion in crushing, increasing density, increasing acceleration to form a mass.

How does Baudrillard conceive these connections and images? The only guide we have is his more general theory, and here it is evident that the whole development of nuclear power and similar technical developments are second order simulations (1987d: 21). In one essay he described it as the model for the new universities, new industrial developments, even for new hypermarkets (which marked the end of the city) (1981a: 113–20). The Beaubourg is thus a confused cultural object, modelled on a technical formation already passé, but turned inside out by the twist of the hyperreal. Even the content of exhibitions at the Beaubourg tends to be thrown back on to the technical forms of the era of production.

Thus Baudrillard does not work towards a single concept of the Thing. His writing appears divided between the attempt to provide a theoretical frame, which identifies the basic opposition between the symbolic order and the order of simulation, a theory of the different orders of simulation and the possibility of a seductive form, a theory of the nature of modern ambience now exploded from its initial limited sphere, and the consequent abolition of interiority, on the one hand. And, on the other, an application to a specific object. The object provides the basic point, focus of unity. It is a single phenomenon, and as it embeds multiple simulations across various orders and dimensions it becomes a complex object. The writing is also a complex combination of theoretical and poetic invention. The 'monological level' is that which identifies the stages of cultural simulation; the poetic or symbolic level is that of the secret attraction of images, the affinities and gravitation between terms. There is also a division between the structural analysis of the Beaubourg as a 'perfect operator' of the circulation of the fluids and masses and a strategic analysis of the struggle over the building, its social forces, and its possible destiny.

The analysis then is more complex than first appears, and can be said to lead to the identification of three contradictions: first is that between the third order simulation of the hyperreal exterior and the culture of the interior; the second contradiction is a social contradiction between the strategy of the élite for the acculturation of the masses and the actual consequences of the Beaubourg; and third, there is that between the real potential of the building in terms of a culture appropriate to the phase of simulation (which he defines as Borgesian) and the actual culture (anti-culture) of the Beaubourg.

THE BONAVENTURE HOTEL: BAUDRILLARD AND JAMESON

Curiously, Baudrillard's ferocious critique of the Beaubourg had much of its impact at one remove, in the debate over the Bonaventure Hotel in Los Angeles, via Fredric Jameson's paper, 'Postmoderism: the cultural logic of late capitalism' (1984a). An analysis of the main differences between these two analyses is instructive. Baudrillard began his analysis with the question: what is this thing? Jameson believes the Bonaventure 'is a popular building, visited with enthusiasm by locals and tourists alike . . . there are two entrances to the Bonaventure, one from Figueroa, and the other two by way of elevated gardens on the other side'. Baudrillard immediately sees 'a carcass', a series of contradictions, fatal strategies. Jameson leads to a suggestion 'about these curiously unmarked ways-in . . . they seem to have been imposed by a new strategy of closure governing the inner space of the hotel itself . . . the Bonaventure aspires to being a total space'.

Let us say that the modes of conceptualization and of writing are strikingly opposed. Baudrillard is arrogant, brash, dogmatic, assertive, fast, brilliant; Jameson is qualified, leisurely, hesitant ('now I want to say a few words about escalators . . . I am more at a loss when it comes to conveying the thing itself'). The conclusions also are remarkedly different. Baudrillard calls for the masses to destroy the building from within, sacrificially. Jameson suggests a discrepancy, 'an alarming disjunction' between body experience and the built environment and proposes to write a new 'mapping' of postmodern space (see 'Cognitive mapping', in Nelson and Grossberg (1988: 347–60) which begins 'I am addressing a subject about which I know nothing whatsoever . . .'). Yet the striking result has been that Baudrillard's essay in Jameson's hands has become an exercise in postmodernism, or deeply associated with it. In reality Baudrillard's essay was profoundly anti-modernist, basing itself on the values of a culture of symbolic exchange and ritual, in alliance with a mass which 'consciously' wanted to destroy culture (Baudrillard's pataphysics), and Jameson's essay took this as a model and simulated its critical style.

But first of all Jameson was immediately criticized for confusing high modernism with postmodernism in architecture (see Shumway, in Kellner 1989c: 192), something that Baudrillard never does, but above all he was criticized for having missed the social significance of the Bonaventure: 'far from eliminating the last enclaves of pre-capitalist production', postmodern capitalism 'has brazenly recalled the most primitive forms of urban exploitation. At least 100,000 homeworkers toil within a few miles radius of the Bona-venture' (Davis 1985: 110). And Davis points out the explicit social dynamic of buildings like the Bonaventure, set in a downtown 'beseiged landscape . . . what is missing in Jameson's otherwise vivid description of the Bonaventure is the savagery of its insertion' in the city, to speak of its 'popular character' is to miss the point of its systematic segregation from the great Hispanic-Asian city outside' (Davis 1985: 112, a point also made by Shumway (in Kellner 1989c) and by Jaccoby 1987: 171). What is remarkable, says Davis, is the way in which the Bonaventure seems to be a bourgeois, high-security simulation of the genuinely popular spaces outside. What Davis provides, echoing Baudrillard's essay on the Beaubourg, is the evocation of the Bonaventure as a 'claustro-phobic space colony attempting to miniature nature within itself': outside there is vibrant but lower-class culture. In quite a different spirit from Jameson, Davis concludes that postmodern architecture is 'little more than a decadent trope of a massified modernism, a sympathetic correlate to Reaganism and the end of urban reform' (Davis 1985: 113).

Others have criticized even the idea that the space in the Bonaventure is anything new – it is surely just another modernist internationalism, says Shumway, and continues: the assertion that it is a hyperspace, a suppression of depth is quite erroneous: it 'contains enormous depth; what it lacks . . . are surfaces'. All the other effects and experiences are modernist clichés. In effect, says Shumway, Jameson fails to distinguish any specific elements of postmodernism, except a certain eclecticism.

Other commentators tend to agree with Davis, although one important contribution points to the fact that Davis says nothing about the cultural dimensions of struggle at all, the strategic urban problem is everything. Cooke (1988) defines postmodernism as a deformed critique of high-modernist élitism, a populist decentring. Thus the debate which took off from the Beaubourg ends with the question of the validity of Jameson's notion of postmodernism. But it is not quite the end, since, remarkably, Baudrillard has re-entered the debate. He visited the Bonaventure and wrote up a short note on his experience in his book *America*. This is one of the occasions when, probably quite fortuitously, the author himself can be called to give his judgement (like the appearance of McLuhan himself in a cinema queue just at the moment Woody Allen was arguing over the interpretation of one of his books: convenient for Woody Allen who could call in the expert himself to confirm his own point of view). Would Baudrillard confirm Jameson's reading of the Bonaventure, or Davis's, Shumway's, or indeed Cooke's?

Baudrillard's note of his visit to the Bonaventure is, on first appearance, nothing remotely like his bitter attack on Beaubourg. He begins, not at an entrance, but at the top, at the summit in the cocktail bar (and no doubt has a drink): something is moving, what is it, he asks, the windows, the building, the world? A dizzy feeling (*sentiment vertigineux*) overwhelms him, he notes, 'which continues inside the Hotel as a result of its labyrinthine convolutions (in space)'. (David Harvey suggests this is a fundamental feature of postmodernism, a cultivation 'of the labyrinthine qualities of urban environments . . . through the creation of an interior sense of inescapable complexity, and interior maze' – and cites the Bonaventure (Harvey 1989: 83)). He stops and ask rhetorically 'is this gadget postmodern architecture' (Baudrillard 1986: 59; 1988a: 59, translation modified in order to make the reference to the gadget clear), 'is this still architecture?' The glass façade functions here, he says, like dark glasses which hide the eyes 'and others see only their own reflection' – this goes for the whole structure of this building, 'the transparency of interfaces ends in internal refraction'. Like the individual in the modern world of so-called 'communication', who is more and more a self-contained monad, in his 'artificial immunity', the Bonaventure Hotel 'cuts itself off from the city'. It 'stops seeing it [and] refracts it like a dark surface. And you cannot get out of the building itself. You cannot fathom out its internal space, but it has no mystery.' This puzzle without a mystery is 'like a game where you have to join all the dots . . . here too everything connects, without two eyes ever meeting.' Baudrillard moves outside – 'it is the same . . . a camouflaged individual, with a long beak . . . wanders along the sidewalks downtown, and nobody, but nobody looks at him. . . . Everything is charged with a somnambulic violence and you must avoid contact to escape its potential discharge' (1988a: 59–60).

Thus within the space of a couple of paragraphs Baudrillard has in fact covered all the points in the debate: the question of depth (the dizzy bar experience), disorientation (but what Baudrillard misses in the Bonaventure is not some new cognitive mapping, but the mystery, the secret), surfaces, and he even muses over the question of the postmodern. A claustrophobia, the self-sufficient city. He does not find the life outside a vibrant exciting community, but a desolation, a latent violence, a latent hysteria. The image of the mass here is therefore quite different from the one in the Beaubourg; here, the desire to make contact, to touch, is inverted, contact is avoided for fear of consequences. Everything here is transparent; however, this is an illusion for the impression is that the environment is a two-way mirror – as if you are being watched while you see only your own reflection.

The structure of imagery in this short passage is remarkable, just as it was in *The Beaubourg Effect*. The dominant mode is visual, not tactile, the eye is all important:

1. at the apex, the paradox: 'I get to see the whole city revolve around the top of the hotel';
2. the descent into the 'box of spatio-temporal tricks, ludic and hallucinogenic';

3. the glass façade reflects its own environment: the illusion of surveillance, 'the other can only see his own reflection' (trs. mod.), the experience of claustrophobia;

4. for individuals, wearing dark reflector glasses has the same effect, the individual retreats into his or her own niche, 'into the shadow of his or her own formula . . . artificial immunity' (trs. mod.);

5. buildings like the Bonaventure cut themselves off from their environment: 'they stop seeing it';

6. 'they refract it like a dark surface';

7. the building is a puzzle without a secret, everything connects, 'without any two pairs of eyes ever meeting';

8. outside an eccentric, 'nobody looks at him'.

There is in the short visit to the Bonaventure a remarkable echo of the implosive black hole of the Beaubourg, but here experienced as descent. Baudrillard begins in the light, at the cocktail bar, it is spinning (Baudrillard's light humour, after a visit to the bar the world revolves around him), and he becomes dizzy. In the Jamesonian fashion he becomes disorientated (but he is pissed): he descends into the world of dark surfaces and reflector dark glasses.

It is remarkable, if we turn back to Jameson's account, that the image of the dark glasses also made its appearance:

the glass skin repels the city outside; a repulsion for which we have analogies in those reflector sunglasses which make it impossible for your interlocutor to see your own eyes and thereby achieve a certain aggressivity towards and power over the Other. In a similar way, the glass skin achieves a peculiar and placeless dissociation of the Bonaventure from its neighbourhood: it is not even an exterior, in as much as when you seek to look at the Hotel's outer walls you cannot see the Hotel itself, but only the distorted images of everything that surrounds it.

(Jameson 1984a)

In this passage the images are not articulated, and tend to begin to contradict each other:

1. the glass façade is a glass skin which repels the city;

2. the repulsion is in the form of a reflection;

3. if you are wearing reflector sunglasses you can achieve aggressivity and power over the Other;

4. the glass skin effectively dissociates the building from its environment;

5. this skin is not a true exterior and enables the building to disappear in the reflection of the world outside.

The two accounts do have some points in common, but what is striking are the differences. This is an important confrontation since we are, for the first time, faced with the problem of the assessment of fiction-theory. Clearly there is no correct, or true, answer here as to whether the Bonaventure is glass skin or not, and all epistemologies of the theory-fact, as opposed to theory-fiction, are rendered inappropriate. A comparison between the two accounts is instructive.

First, Baudrillard's dominant image achieves a remarkable unity, whereas Jameson's glass skin which repels by reflection is awkward, a simple tautology if the skin is mirror-like, and doesn't develop the theme of the skin itself. Second, Baudrillard connects the dark glasses with the theme of the monad, and with the building as monad. Jameson never achieves this connection, for he suggests links around the idea of the glass skin which repels the city, makes it possible to attain power over the other (the city?), and makes it possible to disappear (the idea of repulsion in the form of disappearance is contradictory). Third, Baudrillard's point of view is from the outside, as an outsider: 'people wear dark glasses. Their eyes are hidden'. But Jameson is an insider: 'reflection sunglasses which make it impossible for your interlocutor to see your own eyes and thereby achieve a certain aggressivity towards and power over the Other'. In effect, Jameson here directly identifies with the aggressor, and with the aggressivity of the building itself, whereas Baudrillard is, in the last resort, its victim. Fourth, Baudrillard suggests a mode of surveillance over the individual who is forced into a niche (cf. the space in the Beaubourg, each in his or her bubble), but his view over the city itself from the Bonaventure is from the summit, and as an ironically egoistic tourist; from the main part of the Bonaventure the city cannot be seen: it stops seeing the city: Jameson implies the building's surveillance over the city. Fifth, Baudrillard links the atomistic individualism of the masses inside with those outside; Jameson notes from the outside, 'when you look at the Hotel's outer walls you cannot see the Hotel itself' – is he speaking as tourist, analyst, from the point of view of the people? No doubt all three, just as it is for Baudrillard. Sixth, for Baudrillard there is a torrent of theoretical observation made deftly through the use of rapid references to the gadget, to ambience, dark surface, puzzle without secret, the monad's niche, the escape of the mad, latent hysteria, and building to a devastating irony: this is the ideal city – there really is no one behind these dark glasses, they are only façades, just as there is no one behind the reflector sunglasses in the street (the screen performs the illusion of surveillance by ironically invoking the ideal city for the ruling élite – a city with no people). Jameson evokes the dialectical puzzle of the exterior glass skin which by repelling the external world enables it to disappear into it.

Although these comparisons concern imagery, metaphor, and are in the realm of fiction-theory, it is still possible to assess their effectiveness both in terms of aesthetic power and in terms of their political and theoretical positions. It is Baudrillard's very rapid account which is more effective, forceful, unified, and evocative, even in its humour, its wit. Underlying these images are vast processes of theoretical labour which are condensed into them: indeed these images function to detonate these theories developed at another level, to reactivate them, to make them live.

For Mike Davis the Bonaventure is a bourgeois simulation of the vibrant culture of the city, but Baudrillard's vision is altogether different. He descends from the cocktail bar, suitably dizzy, loses himself in the maze of the dark interior, and escapes into the outside world.

But what does he meet? Not Davis's vibrant community, but 'a camouflaged individual, with a long beak, feathers, and a yellow cagoule, a madman in fancy dress . . . and nobody but nobody looks at him . . .' (1988a: 60) except Baudrillard who recognizes another outsider.

Chapter 12

Conclusion
The other Baudrillard

Baudrillard remains enigmatic, a figure with his own form of solitude, struggling in the void between symbol and simulation (is that not the destiny of critical intellectuals?). Yet some of the features of his project are becoming more visible to us. He is not always capable of surprising and provoking us to the degree he would wish, and some of his analyses are vulnerable to the most harsh of judgements. Yet the overall impression we are left with is of a consistency and persistence of critical imagination which produces, sometimes, remarkable insights. Some of his work is utterly self-defeating, even hypocritical. But there is an undeniable vitality and creativity coupled with an undying fidelity not to a utopian vision in a passive sense, but to a passionate utopian practice in theory. He is no strategist, but an ultraleftist whose Gods are barely recognizable. Like Mahler, whose music is interrupted by strange festive outbursts, Baudrillard's works suddenly lurch into a violent pataphysical mode. They have a black humour, and what are we if we cannot laugh?

But there is another side to Baudrillard. He is the author of remarkable investigations into consumer society, and in his earlier works made important contributions to Marxist and critical theory (which were largely ignored outside France). His works since the mid-1970s, on the basis of a reorganized problematic, began to find the same phenomena repeated endlessly everywhere: possibly the sign that the world was becoming homogeneous, possibly because his modes of analysis were unable to find the world's diversity and heterogeneity. But he did find one example: the Pompidou Centre, the 'Beaubourg', which was analysed as a subtle combination of forms and cultural contradictions. Another was his eventual study *America*, which again found in a single object, great diversity and heterogeneity. At the same time certain other basic changes were taking place in his conceptualization of modern society which seem to suggest that a utopian theoretical practice will in the end produce cruel new analyses of contemporary cultural formations.

These analyses cannot and will not be acceptable to a community founded on ideals of social equality, charity, social support, reciprocity, law, critical political ecology, citizenship, racial and sexual equality. Baudrillard's attitude is that, whether or not these have been achieved, they are a fatally flawed vision of utopia, a sentimental paradise, which shield the social world from its cruel realities.

But is this postmoderism?

Clearly, throughout this examination of Baudrillard the term postmodernism has never been an issue, let alone a central issue. yet, for many, Baudrillard is the postmodern philosopher, the post-modern social theorist *par excellence*, the 'postmodern scene', or the 'high priest of postmodernism'. Baudrillard rarely uses the term, but when he does he is hostile. Labelled a postmodernist, Baudrillard insists he has 'nothing to do with postmodernism' (in Gane 1990). This became evident in fact in a paper delivered to a conference called 'The End of the World', held in New York in 1985, and in his reflections on the term, and phenomenon, in *Cool Memories*. This position seems completely consistent with ironic relation to structuralism and poststructuralism. In fact he turned the concepts and the values of poststructuralism ironically into a symptom of the catastrophe of modern social sciences. The irony has rebounded for this anti-modernist, and anti-postmodernist: he has been caught in the hype of postmoderism. Everywhere he has been identified as the leader, the spokesman of postmodern analysis.

Yet:

As in a general entropic movement of the century, the initial energy is disintegrating ponderously into ever more refined ramifications of structural, pictorial, ideological, linguistic, psychoanalytic upheavals – the ultimate configuration, that of 'postmodernism', undoubtedly the most degenerated, most artificial, and most eclectic phase – a fetishism of picking out and adopting all the significant little bits and pieces, all the idols, and the purest signs that preceded this fetishism.

(Baudrillard 1989a: 40–41, and see 1990c: 149–50)

Baudrillard has subsumed postmodernist thought itself under the object system, as its 'ultimate configuration'. It is certainly a completely coherent and logical analysis: the combinatory begins to tear down, and to permit the interchange, the conversion of whole sectors of culture into a single matrix. But, as with feminism, socialism, and the movements for equality, this configuration is soft and easy. In *Cool Memories* a section of the New York paper is inserted:

> Human rights, dissidence, antiracism, SOS-this, SOS-that: these are soft, easy, *post coitum historicum* ideologies, 'after the orgy' ideologies for an easy going generation which has known neither hard ideologies nor radical philosophies. The ideology of a generation which is neo-sentimental in its politics too, which has rediscovered altruism, conviviality, international charity and the individual bleeding heart . . . soft values condemned by the Nietzschean, Marxo-Freudian age (but also the age of Rimbaud, Jarry and the Situationists). A new generation, that of the spoilt children of the crisis, whereas the preceding one was that of the accursed children of history.
>
> (Baudrillard 1990c: 223–4)

Thus Baudrillard's general perspectives on the twentieth century and its culture begin to emerge very clearly (against the current interpretation of his work). Instead of the break, the transition from modernism to postmodernism, the break or, rather, the intermission was the period of the 1960s and 1970s, which 'opened a gap' in the culture: this is now closing again with postmodernism. Postmoderism, for Baudrillard, is the effect of the continuing action of the mechanisms of uniformity and homogenization, of the feminization of the entire culture; that is, the completion of the project of moderism (thus he is paradoxically closer than imagined to a position such as that of Habermas – who is also against postmodernism).

Again, a brief fragment from the New York conference is contained in *Cool Memories*, and this epitomizes Baudrillard's contempt for postmodernism:

> Postmodernity is the simultaneity of the destruction of earlier values and their reconstruction. It is renovation within ruination. In terms of periods, it is the end of final evaluations and the movement of transcendence, which are replaced by 'teleonomic'

evaluations, in terms of retroaction. Everything is always retro-active, including and, indeed, particularly including – informa-tion. The rest is left to the acceleration of values by technology (sex, body, freedom, knowledge).

(Baudrillard 1990c: 171; cf. 1989a: 43)

In 1984 Fredric Jameson (1984b) attempted to chart the different perspectives on modernism and postmodernism. We are now in a position to locate Baudrillard into the scheme:

	Anti-Modernist	Pro-Modernist
Pro-Postmodernist	Jencks	Lyotard
Anti-Postmodernist	Baudrillard Tafuri	Habermas

He is not alone in his box.

They had taken out such a good insurance policy that when their house in the country burnt down, they were able to build another one older than the first.

(Baudrillard 1990c: 199)

Notes

1 Introduction: the double infidelity

1 A query to Baudrillard as to whether an analysis of his poems, *L'Ange de Stuc*, could be made in terms of Saussurean anagrams, elicited the fact that, although published in the mid-1970s, they were written in the 1950s, when he was interested in Hölderlin. 'I still am', he continued (personal communication, January 1990).
2 Increasingly the preferred mode, as for Nietzsche, is the aphorism, as exemplified in *Cool Memories*. 'The real joy of writing lies in the joy of being able to sacrifice a whole chapter for a single phrase' (Baudrillard 1990c: 29).
3 For an interesting account of recent cultural studies in Britain which contextualizes the moment of Baudrillard's arrival, see Tony Dunn, in Punter (1986: 71–91).

2 From literary criticism to fiction-theory

1 It is certainly curious that this idea, so strikingly evoked in this review, outlines what will become a major theme in Baudrillard's own later work: transpolitical figures.
2 It is also important to note the already highly developed fusion of Dostoevskian and psychoanalytic themes, and the approach to the question of evil, against the background of the importance of historical complexity.
3 Note, however, that Ballard himself revised this view in an interview of 1982: 'I felt that I was not altogether honest in this introduction because I did imply that there was a sort of moral warning which I don't really think is there' (see Benison 1984: note 41).
4 Baudrillard is not altogether consistent in his later writings on this point, since he writes elsewhere on the importance of maintaining the imagery of pathology, of perversion, as a conceptual tool in this phase of simulation, whereas Ballard loses it.
5 Pataphysical mode: the science of imaginary solutions according to Alfred Jarry (see LaBelle 1980).
6 Benison remarks that Baudrillard's reading 'comes perilously close to

making of Ballard's book a rather trite allegory achieved by literary tricks. . . . At this level of "lived ideology" (if I may call it that) Baudrillard sees a message for those who wish to eliminate all the black areas of the map of knowledge' (Benison 1984: 39).

7 For a different use of Borges's highly charged fiction-theory itself in the mode of fiction-pastiche, see my 'Borges: Menard: Spinoza' (in Gane 1989: 137–51).

8 This use of the term 'total simulation' raises problems of consistency of terminology. Baudrillard's use of the term 'symbolic exchange' in primitive societies seems on one level to suggest that these cultures are dominated by other structures than those of simulation. But here, and elsewhere, it is clear that there is a synchronic total simulation as double, the relation to the double is quite different from that found in modern simulations, for 'the primitive has a duel not an alienated relation with his double' (1976: 217). This terminology is clarified in *Seduction*, with the genealogy of the duel, the polarity, and digitality, as forms of play within simulation. It is important to correct here Kaplan's interpretation. She says, 'By "simulacra" Baudrillard means a world in which all we have are simulations, there being no "real" external to them, no "original" that is being copied. It is as if all were reduced merely to exteriors, there no longer being any "interiors" ' (in Pribram 1988: 155). This should be corrected to suggest that 'reality' is a particular form of simulacrum produced in western culture in the rupture of the symbolic order. When the 'real' as a particular simulacrum of a specific historical period itself disappears (along with the dialectic, history, 'man'), a new phase of simulation occurs, the *hyperreal*, since the 'referent' is no longer imagined as the 'exterior' (though it was a simulacrum), but as the model, 'interior' to culture (but one which dissolves the border zones, and the order of law, and thus paradoxically approaches the schizophrenic state of utter loss of the subject into total exteriority), the triumph of the code, and the structural law of value. Kaplan's summary chart (ibid. 1988: 133) of Baudrillard's scheme conflates the period and characteristics of the historical phase, for Baudrillard the hot, explosive phase, with that of the phase of symbolic order itself. Thus Kaplan produces a scheme that is quite remote from that of Baudrillard.

3 Modern ambience of objects

1 The first in 1970 (see Baudrillard 1988b: 33) and the second in 1987 (see Baudrillard 1988c: 91). There is in fact no contradiction here – the object system undoubtedly is a 'structuralist phenomenology!' But there are lingering temptations still in this direction.

2 It is extraordinary that Douglas Kellner, after having been in debate with Baudrillard for many years, could still write that it is important to distinguish true and false needs: 'needs are false if they are commodities which people do not really need or if they rest on expectations and make promises that can be demonstrated to be false' (1989b: 159). Kellner seems happy with this tautology.

3 There is little doubt that Baudrillard at this stage adopted these terms in a positive manner, that, as Barthel (1988: 33) points out, he develops a theory of phantamataic, differential, and sacrificial logic. But, as Barthes himself does not develop a conception of the latter and generalizes the differential logic universally, it is apparent that Baudrillard tends to move against Barthes, towards an ironic critique of the semiological combinatory. In the last instance Schor is probably right to argue that Barthes' position 'is diametrically opposed to that of Baudrillard; in the *Fashion System* he [Barthes] enthusiastically praises just the sort of detail despised by those who yearn after the lost object' (1987: 57). Nevertheless there is still a suspicion that the operation of semiology here also tends to find a certain homogeneity in things. 'The system of (historical social) needs now becomes less coherent than the system of objects themselves', says Baudrillard (1968: 222).

4 Miller (1987) tries, in his influential book, to come to terms with Baudrillard, but never succeeds in grasping Baudrillard's position.

5 Culler's well-known critique of Barthes – that his method in *The Fashion System* was fundamentally flawed since it could not deal with diachronic processes (1975: 35) – is, clearly, not a criticism which can be levelled at Baudrillard. The problem in Baudrillard is that the specifically structuralist concepts of diachrony and system have little actual effectiveness in Baudrillard's analytical writing.

6 This theme, collection, is discussed by Baudrillard, with reference to the film *The Collector* (1965: William Wyler), in *Seduction* (1990a). There is relatively little research on this theme, but see the interesting discussion, obviously aware of the object system, in the chapter 'On collecting art and culture', in Clifford 1988 (215–51).

4 Technology and culture

1 See McLuhan (1967). The debate on McLuhan in Stearn (1969) is still informative, as is Jonathan Miller's *McLuhan* (1971) which has to be read against McLuhan's bitter counter-criticisms: Miller 'prefers argument to enlightenment' and his critique is a 'motivated somnambulism', which presents McLuhan through 'bureaucratic categories' (McLuhan 1987: 436, 442–5). McLuhan, like Baudrillard, who seems to have been enlightened by McLuhan, suggests the importance of aphorism as a mode of theoretical investigation. Eco, in a review of 1967, makes some crucial critical points, especially the analysis of McLuhan's mode of exposition as 'a deliberate regeneration of terminology for provocatory purposes' (Eco 1986: 233). A comparison of the reviews of Baudrillard and Eco in this period is highly instructive as to the orientation of two versions of semiology. Eco is more rationalist, Baudrillard interested in complex historical formations.

2 See section one, 'Lefebvre and the Situationists' (by Lefebvre, Blanchot, Edward Ball, and G. Ulmer) in Kaplan and Ross 1987.

5 The rigours of consumer society

1 And Baudrillard discusses at length popular sociological and economic analyses of consumerism and affluence, by Galbraith, Reisman, Boorstin, Packard, but, although he was translator of Brecht, he does not situate the discussion in relation to the writings of German Marxism, especially those of the Frankfurt School.

2 Following a very similar line to that of the Durkheimian critique of utilitarianism.

3 This formulation attempts and effects a massive and extraordinary unification of the Althusserian and Frankfurt School problematic, and implies a critique of both, certainly against the Althusserian discussion of fetishism as a purely intellectual or ideological field of misrecognitions. For Baudrillard it is a more strongly defined site of social discipline, now through paradoxical forms of gratification and inner repression, a move in society itself from a strategy of physical discipline to one through play and pleasure.

4 One of the most highly structuralist versions of the theory of interpellation under the conditions of advanced capitalism.

5 In the book, *The Object System*, it was the signs which were consumed, here Baudrillard shifts dramatically towards the Althusserians.

6 In his contribution to *Reading Capital* (Althusser and Balibar 1970), Balibar noted the purely epistemological parallel between Freud and Marx: Marx's theory of the displacement of the dominant instance, from politics to economics, and Freud's notion of the displacement in sexual maturation of the erogenous zones. Baudrillard greatly intensifies this imagery, but with the irony (taken from Marcuse and Barthes) that instead of following a normal route social evolution follows into paradoxical perversion. Note, also, that, because Baudrillard makes consumption the site of repression, class struggle can no longer have the decisive function of reproduction of relations of production. This is absorbed into the system.

7 This theme is taken up in a later phase of Baudrillard's work, in terms not of personalization but of the mode of formation of the mass itself. It can therefore be seen directly as the continuation of Baudrillard's work in semiology: the ISAs (state ideological apparatuses), especially the mass media, through digitalization, produce a new ideological phenomenon: the public opinion of the masses.

8 As yet there is no satisfactory discussion of Baudrillard and psychoanalysis. The essay by Levin (1984), though interesting in other respects, says very little about Baudrillard's cultural theory and the use of psychoanalysis.

9 Althusser and Balibar (1970: 192–3): 'the very existence of the machinery in its effect.'

10 Thus Baudrillard writes in the shadow not of the masses but of Althusser.

11 This formula is crucial in Baudrillard, see the epigraph to *L'Ange de Stuc* (1978). Here begins the first major elaboration of Baudrillard's version of the Nietzschean theme of *ressentiment*, expressed here in psychoanalytic terms.

12 Baudrillard makes dramatic use of the theme of the double, particularly versions of Chamisso's story (1814 [1979]) of Peter Schlemihl, who sold his shadow in exchange for the infinite purse of Fortunatus, only to find he was reviled by humanity. He is offered a further exchange, his shadow will be returned if he exchanges his soul. He refuses, and with the aid of seven-league boots, devotes himself to science and useful work to compensate his loss. Other stories in this genre include Hans Andersen's 'The Shadow', in which the shadow returns and inverts the previous relation so that the shadow becomes master: when this humiliation is resisted, the shadow has his former master put to death. Tymms notes 'the process by which this reversal takes place is ingeniously perverse' (1949: 77). See Midgley, 1984: 113–31.

6 From production to reproduction

1 Baudrillard often plays with the idea of a 'mode of seduction', and through this undoubtedly in the last instance ends up himself, half consciously, in society's own 'mirror of seduction', just as Marx found himself in a mirror of production.
2 And even Bataille is soon forced to be radicalized; see Baudrillard (1987e).
3 In fact Baudrillard identifies many such subjects: revolutionaries, poets, blacks, women. Note that Baudrillard's relation to revolution and revolutionaries is not simple. The formal revolutionaries (party, theorists, militants) play a directly counter-revolutionary role in practice by valorizing the importance of production.
4 In effect, another indication of Baudrillard's notion that 'nothing happens' in production; but then this nothing turns out to be quite remarkable.
5 A complete reorganization of the earlier notions of succession of class simulations (bourgeois, petit bourgeois) elaborated in 1972 (1981b). Instead of concentrating on the subject (petit bourgeoisie and social classes), the analysis now moves on to another level of the simulation of objects themselves.
6 At the end of *The Mirror of Production* (Baudrillard 1973), and at the end of his critique of Foucault (*idem* 1987c), he stresses that the system can end 'at a stroke'. In those essays it was the effect of a challenge of symbolic exchange, here it is the very internal fragility of the system. Baudrillard adopts a rigorous utopian practice.
7 The structural terms are used as an index themselves of the changes in society: it is the irony of structuralism which imagined that it had refuted essentialism and the expressive totality.
8 Baudrillard moves towards the ultraleft, or even towards the lumpenproletariat, since it is essential to escape the decomposition of the proletariat and the process of normalization. The position of the outsider is essential for the theorist if he or she is to remain in any sense radical. To take up a proletarian position today means to adopt the attitude of reproduction of work (see another discussion of this in Gorz

1990). But the revolutionary challenge is from today's outsider groups and these ally themselves to the symbolic orders (ironically he does not apply the same exclusion model to women, unlike Durkheim (1963), who on this score is more radical than Baudrillard, already having his first exclusions, with the fundamental exclusion of women (Gane 1983b)).

9 This attack on the unions was part of a widespread reaction in the 1970s in France, a reaction specifically against the role of the communist-led CGT and the PCF itself in the failure of 1968. Like Baudrillard, Foucault also identified the unions and communists as 'bureaucrats of the revolution' (in Deleuze and Guattari 1977: xii). Some of the ironic (and non-ironic) openings this allowed intellectuals on the left to develop against Marxism an increasingly anti-communist ideology is discussed by Dews in Gane 1986 (61–105).

10 Curiously, Baudrillard repeats this piece of advertising sloganeering in his book *America* as if he found it there too.

11 I use the term from Hubert and Mauss (1964).

12 The idea of revolution here completely changes its meaning in Baudrillard. Instead of the revolution as the triumph of accumulation, of reason, of labour of the negative, it is the irruption of the reversible time of symbolic exchange. With this stroke Baudrillard has taken Foucault's own analyses of genealogy into Bataille's field of sacrificial analysis where they can be used to explain the process of the destruction of the symbolic in production (which still thereby retains a centrality).

13 It is at this point that Baudrillard moves from Mauss's beneficent to Nietzsche's maleficent notion of symbolic exchange, under the influence at this moment of Bataille.

14 Lukes has argued that there is no Durkheimian theory of power (1973), but it can be seen that Mauss discovered a theory of power within Durkheim's work which was to have enormous ramifications in French theory. Some interpretations discover this idea through Nietzsche and then in Baudrillard himself. Kroker has argued that what Baudrillard then does is to insert Nietzsche's cynical will to power into Marx's *Capital*: 'Capital is the reverse but parallel image of the will to power', '. . . on the downside of the will to power, the side of a cynical, infinite regress into disaccumulation, disintegration, and darkness, Capital can make its reappearance as the master text of the will to power on the side of power/seduction without limit' (Kroker 1988: 181). This argument is entirely misleading, and creates a new status for Capital out of all proportion to Baudrillard's project. The theory of *ressentiment* is not inserted into Marx, as is clear in the non-class terminology adopted (mass, élite). Kroker ends his comment with a parody of Baudrillard, a sheer panic (babble) theory: Baudrillard has revealed the existence of a will to will, as the third term, the abstract unity, which makes the mirror of production of totality, and lends to the fiction of Capital, the 'double-metamorphosis' of the commodity form, 'a certain abstract coherency'. If this means that the will to will produces both Marxist theory and the code of commodity exchange, then Kroker is certainly in error, for Baudrillard's point is that Marx was caught in the code, not that it was produced by the same forces.

7 Modernity, simulation, and the hyperreal

1 See the Weberian point of view in Abercrombie *et al.* (1986).
2 Discussions of Baudrillard's notion of simulation are particularly disappointing. Charles Levin, for example, in his introduction to extracts from Baudrillard (in Fekete 1984: 46–53) talks about everything except simulation. Clearly, Baudrillard's genealogy of simulation is closely related to that constructed by Foucault; see Major-Poetzl (1983) and Gutting (1989) for resumés in a form which permit immediate comparison – for example with Baudrillard as presented by Chen (1987: 72–7), though Chen converts Baudrillard's genealogy into a scheme of modernity–postmodernity quite out of line with Baudrillard's own thought (compare Chang 1986: 162–8). Foucault's notion of the imminent death of 'Man' is reflected in its turn in Baudrillard's death of the social, as if to reveal that each of Foucault's projects leads to more fundamental problems. The whole project of the genealogy of simulations is a major reworking of Baudrillard's first problematic of cultural class strategies. Under the influence of Foucault, all elements of class struggle have been removed, leading to the appearance of an immense superstructural process without agency, a 'process without a subject'. It is a completely new problematic, a changed notion of the location of power (no longer in the grip of a hidden ruling class), a changed conception of the cultural system, and a transformed notion of the current situation as one of increasingly perverse structuration, in which the proletariat, unlike other previously oppressed groups, is no longer excommunicated. Against the analysis earlier of the structural ambivalence of the petit bourgeoisie, the new ambivalence is that of the working class itself as it now seeks to play its part in reproducing work for the sake of work.
3 In fact Baudrillard's position is very much dominated by a fusion of Derrida, Bataille, Foucault, and McLuhan. Note Benjamin's consideration of allegory as simulation in baroque theatre (and Lukacs's interesting critique (1978)), his conception of surrealism (Benjamin 1978, and in 1979), as well as his well-known essay on art and mechanical reproduction (in 1968), all clearly part of a project directly parallel to that of Baudrillard. But note also the decisive influence of McLuhan, whose work Baudrillard read in a way that was extremely faithful to McLuhan's own reflections: the phrase the 'medium is the message' has to read, McLuhan said, as the effective creation of new environments, 'always invisible until they have been superseded by new environments' (1987: 465).
4 This analysis of modern art has given rise to a considerable debate, for art theorists are both attracted to it and bemused by it. A good example is the comment by David Carrier, 'The ultimate value of Baudrillard's analysis is to project with nightmarish consistency a vision of art which I find repugnant . . . even Baudrillard's bitterest enemies are indebted to this working out of an extreme position' (Carrier 1988: 60). Carrier provides a useful corrective to the interpretation by Hal Foster and Fredric Jameson, and finds himself, with great embarrassment, having written a book which 'is – I now recognise – uncannily Baudrillardian'.

8 Fashion, the body, sexuality, and death

1 This is, in effect, Baudrillard's genealogy of modern narcissicism, part
   of a genealogy of sexuality in general, parallel with other genealogies
   based on the early exemplars of Foucault. Baudrillard himself was
   clearly disconcerted when Foucault turned to sexuality only to work out
   a completely different form of history from his own. It is also important
   to note that, although Baudrillard recognizes part of the 'confinement'
   of women historically, he is never 'extreme' here. It appears as if they
   enter the system and are 'emancipated' rather like proletarians in a
   highly ambiguous form, and become subject to the process of normalization with its defusing of radical potentialities.
2 This concept of narcissicism is crucial to Baudrillard's account of
   modern culture. There is a parallel account in the influential work of
   Lasch (1980: 31–51), on which see the debate in *Salamundi* 1979 (no.
   46) and the essay by Altieri in O'Hara 1985.
3 Kellner notes: 'In these analyses he combines some insightful, often
   brilliant, Foucaultian genealogies of death as a social construct in
   different historical epochs with a Derridean deconstruction of the
   antinomy of life and death in Western thought' (Kellner 1989a: 102–5).
4 For an account of mortuary rituals, see Huntington and Metcalf (1979);
   for a detailed study of death and symbolic exchange see 'Death as
   exchange: two Melanesian cases' by Strathern (in Humphreys and King
   1981: 205, 223).
5 As Aries says, death becomes 'shameful and forbidden' (1976).
6 This is an important preparation for the analysis of the specific modification of the theory of simulation, for later Baudrillard suggests these
   societies exist always in 'total simulation' as opposed to the single
   hyperreal simulation which eliminates the effect of the uncanny.
7 Baudrillard neglects to say what this might amount to in any serious
   sense.

9 Anagrammatic resolutions

1 The allusion here is to Starobinski's *Les Mots sous Les Mots* (The
   Words under the Words) (1971). Saussure's theses presented by Starobinski have become immensely influential in literary analysis especially
   in poetic analysis, from Bowie's analyses of Mallarmé (1978) and,
   indirectly, to Shamoon Zamir's 'Blake in birdland: displacements and
   metamorphosis in the poetics of Ismael Reed' (in Murray 1989).
2 Which makes this a very dangerous phenomenon to investigate.
   Saussure didn't publish his investigations, perhaps realizing the dangers
   of not just finding but inventing the anagram, as I have done here with
   respect to Baudrillard's poems in order to demonstrate what is at stake.
3 In any case, the anagram technique, if applied, arrives at only a purely
   rational, highly simulatory function, hardly in line with the initiatory
   role it plays in the poetry of antiquity. It would be the equivalent of
   Lacan's highly rationalist advice to psychoanalysts: do crossword

puzzles (Lacan 1968: 29); Baudrillard's advice to utopians would be, do anagrams. Baudrillard's position on poetry is interesting. I have asked Baudrillard: 'I noticed that some of your poems have in part found their way into your prose works. Do you envisage a kind of fusion between poetry and prose in your works?' His response was in English: 'Sure: it is the same game, in other ways. But poetry as such is now impossible, I hope it can be displayed and dispersed through . . . fiction theory (especially in the last books). But it can never be "envisaged", it occurs or not' (personal communication 1990). This is consistent with his position in *Cool Memories*, where in 1982 he marked a change of evaluation: 'Poetry reeks too much of poetry and philosophy too much of philosophy. Each suffers from an abominable redundancy, the one an affectation of diction, the other an affectation of profundity. We find both equally tiresome' (Baudrillard 1990c: 92).

10 Transpolitical objects

1 There is need for some caution here, since his use of these key terms is slightly different from the still limited but growing circulation of terms like transsexual, transracial, even transatlantic. The sense of Baudrillard's use is to evoke that which breaks through a threshold, with a strong sense of escalation or spiral of the worst. The terms were originally inspired by Kristeva.
2 See Gane (1988) for Durkheim on the distinction between anomalie and teratology.
3 This in fact is a key image in Althusser's critique of the crisis of Marxism (1978), but the critique never attains the savage intensity of Baudrillard's evocation.
4 This seems at first sight Baudrillard's own form of involution. But the aphoristic form breaks down the system, and acts like a lightning conductor for the stored-up energy of Baudrillard's vast theoretical thunderstorms.
5 True fatalism in active or passive mood is approached here as determination, ineluctable procession across other determinations, and the mood can be active or passive. But the will to power is here turned against itself (*ressentiment*) at the theoretical not the personal level. In a review of considerable inadequacy, Bauman seems to miss the whole tenor of Baudrillard's interventions, seeing in them only a position 'firmly inside the walls. The outside has long been forgotten . . . there is another choice. To find it one would need to stroll outside on foot' (Bauman 1986: 743). Baudrillard in fact makes the point in *America* that it is by leaving the academic cloisters that he has made an unprecedented leap in his understanding of modern cultures. Such propositions written by social theorists of repute perhaps indicate more than a superficial abyss in contemporary epistemology.
6 This section marks the beginning of Baudrillard's new dramatic personal fusion of event and theory, and theory and poetry. But if there is fusion, there is also fission: the aphorism of *Cool Memories*.

7 The term *sideration* is used by Baudrillard here, and is difficult to trans-
  late. In *America*, where the term is often used, the translator very
  imaginatively tries 'starblasted' and 'astral'. The translation (1988b)
  gives 'shattering'.
8 The basic logic of Baudrillard's genealogies, modelled on Foucault. The
  term terrorism and its forms in modern ideology was an important
  theme in the work of Lefebvre.
9 The emergence of a new problem, or a shift in the problematic towards
  the principle of evil.
10 This section of Baudrillard's book has appeared in an English version
   (1989d).
11 It is above all embarrassing for his own theory which suggests the
   fusion of financial and industrial capital.

11 From the Beaubourg to the Bonaventure Hotel

1 The last section on private radio was cut from the version published in
  1981. For an interesting parallel discussion see Guattari's essay
  'Millions and millions of potential Alices' (1984: 236–41) which also
  ends on a certain high optimism: 'In Bologna and Rome there have
  been kindled the fires of a revolution'.
2 But not in the form suggested by MacDonald (in Frankovits 1984:
  22–7), who *reduces* the 'Baudrillard Effect' to the 'Beaubourg Effect'
  itself.
3 Baudrillard later insisted: 'it is by their very inertia in the ways of the
  social laid out for them that the masses go beyond its logic and its
  limits, and destroy its whole edifice. A destructive hyperconformity
  . . . that has all the appearance of a victorious challenge – no one can
  measure the strength of this challenge, of the reversion exerted on the
  whole system' (1983a: 47). It appears that Baudrillard has plucked a
  victory out of the defeat of May '68 – a defeat he lays elsewhere at the
  door of the workers' organizations (1989b). Perhaps the phrase 'all the
  appearance of a victorious challenge' depends on which spectacles he is
  wearing, since, in 1983, Baudrillard seemed completely resigned to the
  defeat of the masses: the Beaubourg is occupied by the 'incestuous
  virulence of the multitude fallen prey to itself' (1990c: 105).

Bibliography

Note: I have kept these references strictly to a minimum. A more ample bibliography of Baudrillard's publications can be found in Kellner's *Jean Baudrillard* (1989a). But the bibliography here lists some further publications, and publications overlooked by Kellner. I have not sought to indicate all the existing translations where there is duplication, or indeed all the French publications where there is duplication. The bibliography here is simply the working selection that I have used in the writing of this book.

Abercrombie, N., Hill, S., and Turner, B.S. (1986) *Sovereign Individuals of Capitalism*, London: Allen & Unwin.
Adorno, T.W. (1967) *Prisms*, London: Spearman.
—— (1989) *Kierkegaard: Construction of the Aesthetic*, Minneapolis: University of Minnesota Press.
Allison, D. (ed.) (1985) *The New Nietzsche*, London: Verso.
Althusser, L. (1969) *For Marx*, London: Allen Lane.
—— (1971) *Lenin and Philosophy and Other Essays*, London: NLB.
—— (1972) 'Reply to John Lewis', *Marxism Today* October: 310–18; November: 343–9.
—— (1976) *Essays in Self Criticism*, London: NLB.
—— (1978) 'The crisis of Marxism', *Marxism Today* July: 215–20, 227.
—— (1982) *Montesquieu, Rousseau, History*, London: Verso.
—— (1990) *Philosophy and the Spontaneous Philosophy of the Scientists, and other Essays*, London: Verso.
Althusser, L. and Balibar, E. (1970) *Reading Capital*, London: NLB.
Anderson, P. (1983) *In the Tracks of Historical Materialism*, London: Verso.
Angus, I. and Jally, S. (eds) (1989) *Cultural Politics in Contemporary America*, London: Routledge.
Aries, P. (1976) *Western Attitudes towards Death*, London: Boyars.
Baehr, P. (1990) 'The "masses" in Weber's political sociology', *Economy and Society* 19(2): 242–65.

Balibar, E. (1978) 'Irrationalism and Marxism', *New Left Review* 170: 3–20.

—— (1985) 'Marx, the joker in the pack', *Economy and Society* 14(1): 1–27.

Ballard, J.G. (1985) *Crash*, London: Faber.

Barthel, D. (1988) *Putting on Appearances*, Philadelphia: Temple University Press.

Barthes, R. (1964) 'Elements de semiologie', *Communications* 4: 91–135.

—— (1967a) *Elements of Semiology*, London: Cape.

—— (1967b) *Writing Degree Zero*, London: Cape.

—— (1972) *Mythologies*, Frogmore: Granada.

—— (1984) *Camera Lucida*, London: Fontana.

—— (1985) *The Fashion System*, London: Cape.

—— (1988) *The Semiotic Challenge*, New York: Hill & Wang.

Bataille, G. (1985) *Visions of Excess*, Manchester: Manchester University Press.

—— (1988) *The Accursed Share*, New York: Zone.

—— (1989) *The Tears of Eros*, San Francisco: City Lights.

Baudrillard, J. (1962–3a) 'Uwe Johnson: La Frontiere', *Les Temps Modernes*, pp. 1094–107.

—— (1962–3b) 'Les Romans d'Italo Calvino', *Les Temps Modernes*, pp. 1728–34.

—— (1962–3c) 'La Proie des flammes', *Les Temps Modernes*, pp. 1928–37.

—— (1967) 'Compte rendu de Marshall McLuhan: *Understanding Media*', *L'Homme et la Société* 5: 227–30.

—— (1968) *Le Système des objects*, Paris: Denoel.

—— (1969a) 'Le Ludique et le policier', *Utopie* 2–3: 3–15.

—— (1969b) 'La practique sociale de la technique', *Utopie* 2–3, 147–55.

—— (1970) *La Société de consommation*, Paris: Gallimard.

—— (1972) *Pour une critique de l'economie du signe*, Paris: Gallimard. (In translation 1981b.)

—— (1973) *Le Miroir de la production*, Tournail: Casterman. (In translation 1975a.)

—— (1975a) *The Mirror of Production*, St Louis: Telos.

—— (1975b) 'Langages de masse', in *Encylopaedia Universalis*, vol. 17, Paris: Organum, pp. 394–7.

—— (1976) *L'Echange Symbolique et la Mort*, Paris: Gallimard.

—— (1977a) *L'Effet Beaubourg: implosion et dissuasion*, Paris: Galilee. (In translation 1982.)

—— (1977b) *Oublier Foucault*, Paris: Galilee. (In translation 1987c.)

—— (1978a) *L'Ange de stuc*, Paris: Galilee.

—— (1978b) *A l'Ombre des majorities silencieuses, ou la fin du social*, Fontenay-sous-Bois: Cahiers d'Utopie. (In translation 1983a.)

—— (1979) *De la seduction*, Paris: Denoel-Gonthier. (In translation 1990a.)

—— (1981a) *Simulacres et Simulation*, Paris: Galilee.

—— (1981b) *For a Critique of the Political Economy of the Sign*, St Louis: Telos. (Translation of 1972.)

———— (1981c) 'Beyond the unconscious: the symbolic', *Discourse* 3: 60–87. (Part translation of 1976.)

———— (1981d) 'Fatality or reversible imminence: beyond the uncertainty principle', *Social Research* 49(2): 272–93. (Part translation of 1983b.)

———— (1982) 'The Beaubourg effect: implosion and deterrence', *October* 20 (spring): 3–13. (Translation of 1977a.)

———— (1983a) *In the Shadow of the Silent Majorities*, New York: Semiotext(e). (Translation of 1978b.)

———— (1983b) *Les Strategies fatales*, Paris: Grasset.

———— (1983c) 'What are you doing after the orgy?', *Artforum* October: 42–6.

———— (1983d) 'Les Seductions de Baudrillard', interview, *Magazine Littéraire* 193 (March): 80–5.

———— (1983e) *Please Follow Me* (with Sophie Calle, *Suite Venitienne*), Paris: Editions de L'Etoile.

———— (1983f) *Simulations*, New York: Semiotext(e). (Part translation of 1981a.)

———— (1984–5) 'Intellectuals, commitment, and political power', *Thesis Eleven* 10–11: 166–73.

———— (1985a) *La Gauche Divine*, Paris: Grasset.

———— (1985b) 'The masses: the implosion of the social in the media', *New Literary History* 16(3): 577–89.

———— (1986) *Amerique*, Paris: Grasset. (In translation 1988a.)

———— (1987a) *L'Autre par lui-meme*, Paris: Galilee. (In translation 1988c.)

———— (1987b) *Cool Memories*, Paris: Galilee.

———— (1987c) *Forget Foucault*, New York: Semiotext(e). (Translation of 1977b.)

———— (1987d) *The Evil Demon of Images*, Annandale: Power Institute.

———— (1987e) 'When Bataille attacked the metaphysical principle of economy', *Canadian Journal of Political and Social Theory* 11(3): 57–62.

———— (1987f) 'Modernity', *Canadian Journal of Political and Social Theory* 11(3): 63–73.

———— (1987g) 'The year 2000 has already happened', in A. and M. Kroker (eds) (1988) *Body Invaders*, London: Macmillan, pp. 35–44.

———— (1988a) *America*, London: Verso. (Translation of 1986.)

———— (1988b) *Jean Baudrillard: Selected Writings*, Cambridge: Polity.

———— (1988c) *The Ecstasy of Communication*, New York: Semiotext(e). (Translation of 1987a.)

———— (1988d) 'Interview: Jean Baudrillard', *Block* 14: 8–10.

———— (1988e) *Please Follow Me* (With Sophie Calle, *Suite Venitienne*), Seattle: Bay Press. (Translation of 1983e.)

———— (1988f) *Xerox to Infinity*, London: Touchepas.

———— (1989a) 'The anorexic ruins', in D. Kamper and C. Wulf (eds) *Looking Back at the End of the World*, pp. 29–45, New York: Semiotext(e).

———— (1989b) 'The end of production', *Polygraph* 2/3: 5–29. (Part translation of 1976.)

———— (1989c) 'Politics of seduction: interview with Baudrillard', *Marxism Today* January: 54–5.

—— (1989d) 'Panic crash!', in A. Kroker, M. Kroker, and D. Cook (eds) *Panic Encylopaedia*, London: Macmillan, pp. 64–7.

—— (1989e) 'An interview with Jean Baudrillard (Judith Williamson)', *Block* 15: 16–19.

—— (1990a) *Seduction*, London: Macmillan. (Translation of 1979.)

—— (1990b) *La Transparence du mal: essai sur les phenomenes extremes*, Paris: Galilee.

—— (1990c) *Cool Memories*, London: Verso. (Translation of 1987b.)

Bauman, Z. (1986) 'The second disenchantment: review', *Theory, Culture and Society* 5(4): 738–43.

—— (1987) *Legislators and Interpreters: On Modernity, Post-modernity and Intellectuals*, Cambridge: Polity.

—— (1990a) 'From pillars to post', *Marxism Today* February: 20–5.

—— (1990b) 'Dawn of the dead', *Emergency* 5: 48–57.

Benhabib, S. (1984) 'The epistemologies of postmodernism', *New German Critique* 33: 103–36.

Benison, J. (1984) 'Jean Baudrillard on the current state of SF', *Foundation* 32: 25–42.

Benjamin, A. (ed.) (1989) *The Problems of Modernity*, London: Routledge.

Benjamin, W. (1968) *Illuminations*, London: Cape.

—— (1978) 'Surrealism: the last snapshot of the European intelligentsia', *New Left Review* 108: 47–56.

—— (1979) *One Way Street*, London: Verso.

Benton, T. (1984) *The Rise and Fall of Structural Marxism*, London: Macmillan.

Best, S. and Kellner, D. (1991) *Postmodern Theory, Theory and Politics*, London: Macmillan.

Blanchot, M. (1980) *L'Ecriture du desastre*, Paris: Gallimard.

—— (1982) *The Space of Literature*, London: University of Nebraska Press.

Blau, J.R. (1989) *The Shape of Culture*, Cambridge: Cambridge University Press.

Bogard, W. (1987) 'Sociology in the absence of the social: the significance of Baudrillard for contemporary thought', *Philosophy and Social Criticism* 13(3): 227–42.

Borges, J. (1970) *Labyrinths*, Harmondsworth: Penguin.

Bourdieu, P. (1984) *Distinction*, London: Routledge.

Bowie, M. (1978) *Mallarmé and the Art of Being Difficult*, Cambridge: Cambridge University Press.

Brenner, R. (with G. Brenner) (1990) *Gambling and Speculation*, Cambridge: Cambridge University Press.

Buhl, P. (1990) 'America: post-modernity?', *New Left Review* 180: 163–75.

Caillois, R. (1959) *Man and the Sacred*, Glencoe: Free Press.

—— (1962) *Man, Play and Games*, London: Thames & Hudson.

—— (1975) 'The College de Sociologie', *Substance* 11–12: 61–4.

Calvino, I. (1959) *The Baron in the Trees*, New York: Harcourt.

—— (1962) *The Nonexistent Knight and the Cloven Viscount*, New York: Harcourt.

Canetti, E. (1978) *The Human Province*, New York: Seabury.

Canguilhem, G. (1978) *On the Normal and the Pathological*, London: Reidel.

Carrier, D. (1988) 'Baudrillard as philosopher or, the end of abstract painting', *Arts Magazine* 63(1): 52–60.

Carrol, J. (1974) *Breakout from the Crystal Palace*, London: Routledge & Kegan Paul.

Carter, A. (1979) *The Sadeian Woman*, London: Virago.

Caruso, P. (1969) *Conversazioni con Lévi-Strauss, Foucault, Lacan*, Milan: Mursia.

Certeau, Michel de (1984) *The Practice of Everyday Life*, London: University of California Press.

Chamisso, A. von (1979) *Peter Schlemihls Wundersame Geschichte*, Berlin: Verlag der Nation.

Chang, B. (1986) 'Mass, media, mass media-tion: Baudrillard's implosive critique of modern mass-mediated culture', *Current Perspectives in Social Theory* 17: 157–81.

Cheal, D. (1988) 'The postmodern origin of ritual', *Journal for the Theory of Social Behaviour* 18(3): 269–90.

Chen, K.H. (1987) 'The masses and the media: Baudrillard's implosive post-modernism', *Theory, Culture and Society* 4(1): 71–88.

Cixous, H. and Clement, C. (1987) *The Newly Born Woman*, Manchester: Manchester University Press.

Clifford, J. (1988) *The Predicament of Culture*, London: Harvard University Press.

Cohen, J. (1969) 'The philosophy of Marcuse', *New Left Review* 57: 35–52.

Connolly, W.E. (1988) *Political Theory and Modernity*, Oxford: Blackwell.

Cooke, P. (1988) 'Modernity, postmodernity and the city', *Theory, Culture and Society* 5: 475–92.

Culler, J. (1975) *Structuralist Poetics*, London: Routledge & Kegan Paul.

D'Amico, R. (1978) 'Desire and the commodity form', *Telos* 35: 88–122.

—— (1981) *Marx and the Philosophy of Culture*, Gainsville: University of Florida Press.

Davis, M. (1985) 'Urban renaissance and the spirit of postmodernism', *New Left Review* 151: 106–13.

Debord, G. (1987) *Society of the Spectacle*, Rebell Press, Aim Publications.

Deleuze, G. (1983) *Nietzsche and Philosophy*, London: Athlone.

Deleuze, G. and Guattari, F. (1977) *Anti-Oedipus*, New York: Viking.

Derrida, J. (1978) *Writing and Difference*, London: Routledge & Kegan Paul.

—— (1981) *Positions*, London: Athlone.

—— (1987) *The Postcard*, London: University of Chicago Press.

Descombes, V. (1980) *Modern French Philosophy*, Cambridge: Cambridge University Press.

Donzelot, J. (1988) 'The promotion of the social', *Economy and Society* 17(3): 395–427.

Dostoevsky, F. (1972) *Notes from the Underground*, Harmondsworth: Penguin.

Durkheim, E. (1957) *Professional Ethics and Civic Morals*, London: Routledge & Kegan Paul.
—— (1961) *The Elementary Forms of the Religious Life*, New York: Collier.
—— (1963) *Incest: The Nature and Origin of the Taboo*, New York: Lyle Stuart.
—— (1964) *The Division of Labour in Society*, London: Collier-Macmillan.
—— (1972) *Suicide*, London: Routledge & Kegan Paul.
Eagleton, T. (1990) *The Ideology of the Aesthetic*, Oxford: Blackwell.
Eco, U. (1986) *Travels in Hyperreality*, London: Pan.
Elliot, G. (1987) *Althusser: The Detour of Theory*, London: Verso.
Falk, P. (1988) 'The past to come', *Economy and Society* 17(3): 374–94.
Fekete, J. (ed.) (1984) *The Structural Allegory*, Minneapolis: University of Manchester Press.
—— (ed.) (1988) *Life After Postmodernism*, London: Macmillan.
Ferry, L. and Renaut, A. (1985) *La Pensée 68*, Paris: Gallimard.
Forrester, J. (1980) 'Michel Foucault and the history of psychoanalysis', *History of Science* 18.
Foster, H. (1985a) *Recodings: Art Spectacle, Cultural Politics*, Seattle: Bay Press.
—— (ed.) (1985b) *Postmodern Culture*, London: Pluto.
Foucault, M. (1970) *The Order of Things*, London: Tavistock.
—— (1977) *Language, Counter-Memory, Practice*, Ithaca: Cornell University Press.
—— (1983) 'Structuralism and post-structuralism: an interview with M. Foucault', *Telos* 55 (Spring): 195–211.
—— (1989) *Foucault Live (interviews 1966–84)*, New York: Semiotext(e).
Frankovits, A. (ed.) (1984) *Seduced and Abandoned*, Glebe, Australia: Stonemoss publishers.
Gane, M. (1983a) 'Durkheim: the sacred language', *Economy and Society* 12(1): 1–47.
—— (1983b) 'Durkheim: woman as outsider', *Economy and Society* 12: 227–70.
—— (1983c) 'On the ISAs episode', *Economy and Society* 12: 431–67.
—— (1984) 'Institutional socialism and the sociological critique of communism (introduction to Durkheim and Mauss)', *Economy and Society* 113(3): 304–30.
—— (ed.) (1986) *Towards a Critique of Foucault*, London: Routledge.
—— (1988) *On Durkheim's Rules of Sociological Method*, London: Routledge.
—— (ed.) (1989) *Ideological Representation and Power in Social Relations: Literary and Social Theory*, London: Routledge.
—— (1990) 'Ironies of postmodernism: fate of Baudrillard's fatalism', *Economy and Society* 19: 314–31.
—— (1991) *Baudrillard: Critical and Fatal Theory*, London: Routledge.
Gillespie, M. and Strong, T. (eds) (1988) *Nietzsche's New Faces*, London: University of Chicago Press.

Giradin, J-C. (1974) 'Towards a politics of signs: reading Baudrillard', *Telos* 20: 127–37.
Girard, R. (1977) *Violence and the Sacred*, London: Johns Hopkins University Press.
Glucksmann, A. (1972) 'A ventriloquist structuralism', *New Left Review* 72: 68–92.
Goffman, E. (1981) *Forms of Talk*, Oxford: Blackwell.
Gorz, A. (1966) 'Sartre and Marx', *New Left Review* 57: 29–52.
—— (1990) 'The ultimate ideology of work', *Emergency* 5: 13–21.
Gouldner, A.W. (1979) *The Future of Intellectuals*, London: Macmillan.
—— (1980) *The Two Marxisms*, London: Macmillan.
Griffiths, A.P. (ed.) *Contemporary French Philosophy*, Cambridge: Cambridge University Press.
Guattari, F. (1984) *Molecular Revolution*, Harmondsworth: Penguin.
Gutting, G. (1989) *Michel Foucault's Archaeology of Scientific Reason*, Cambridge: Cambridge University Press.
Habermas, J. (1981) 'Modernity versus post modernity', *New German Critique* 22: 3–14.
Harvey, D. (1982) *The Limits to Capital*, Oxford: Blackwell.
—— (1989) *The Condition of Postmodernity*, Oxford: Blackwell.
Hayward, P. (1984) 'Implosive critiques', *Screen* 25: 128–33.
Hebdige, D. (1988) *Hiding in the Light: On Images and Things*, London: Routledge.
Heimonet, J.M. (1984) 'Le College de Sociologie, un gigantesque malentendu', *Esprit* 89: 39–58.
Hirst, P.Q. (1985) *Marxism and Historical Writing*, London: Routledge & Kegan Paul.
Hobsbawm, E. and Ranger, T. (eds) (1984) *The Invention of Tradition*, Cambridge: Cambridge University Press.
Hubert, H. and Mauss, M. (1964) *Sacrifice: Its Nature and Function*, London: Cohen & West.
Humphreys, S. and King, H. (eds) (1981) *Morality and Immortality*, London: Academic Press.
Huntington, R. and Metcalf, P. (1979) *Celebrations of Death*, Cambridge: Cambridge University Press.
Hutchinson, L. (1989) *The Politics of Postmodernism*, London: Routledge.
Huyssen, A. (1986) *After the Great Divide: Modernism, Mass Culture and Postmodernism*, London: Macmillan.
Irigaray, L. (1985) *This Sex which Is Not One*, Ithaca: Cornell University Press.
Jaccoby, R. (1987) *The Last Intellectuals*, New York: Basic Books.
Jameson, F. (1984a) 'Postmodernism, or the cultural logic of late capitalism', *New Left Review* 146: 53–93.
—— (1984b) 'The politics of theory: ideological positions in the postmodern debate', *New German Critique* 33: 53–65.
Jardine, A. (1985) *Gynesis. Configurations of Women and Modernity*, Ithaca: Cornell University Press.
Jencks, C. (1980) *Late-Modern Architecture*, New York: Rizzoli.

Johnson, U. (1963) *Speculations about Jakob*, New York: Harcourt, Brace
    Jovanovich.
Kafka, F. (1967) *America*, Harmondsworth: Penguin.
—— (1979) *Description of a Struggle*, Harmondsworth: Penguin.
—— (1983) *Stories, 1904–24*, London: Macdonald.
Kaplan, A. and Ross, K. (eds) (1987) *Everyday Life* (Yale French Studies,
    73), New Haven: Yale University Press.
Kaye, B. (1989) *A Random Walk Through Fractal Dimensions*, Weinheim:
    VCH.
Kellner, D. (1984) *Herbert Marcuse and the Crisis of Marxism*, London:
    Macmillan.
—— (1987) 'Baudrillard, semiurgy and death', *Theory, Culture and
    Society* 4: 125–46.
—— (1988) 'Postmodernism as social theory', *Theory, Culture and
    Society* 5: 239–69.
—— (1989a) *Jean Baudrillard, From Marxism to Postmodernism and
    Beyond*, Cambridge: Polity.
—— (1989b) *Critical Theory, Marxism and Modernity*, Cambridge:
    Polity.
—— (ed.) (1989c) *Postmodernism, Jameson, Critique*, Washington, DC:
    Maisonneuve Press.
Kelly, M. (1982) *Modern French Marxism*, Oxford: Blackwell.
Kierkegaard, S. (1971) *Either/Or*, vol. 1, New Jersey: Princeton University
    Press.
Kristeva, J. (1980) *Desire in Language*, Oxford: Blackwell.
—— (1986) *The Kristeva Reader*, ed. T. Moi, Oxford: Blackwell.
Kroker, A. (1988) 'Baudrillard's Marx', in *Theory, Culture and Society*
    5: 2–3.
Kroker, A. and Cook, D. (eds) (1988) *The Postmodern Scene*, London:
    Macmillan.
Kroker, A. and Kroker, M. (eds) (1988) *Body Invaders, Sexuality and the
    Postmodern Condition*, London: Macmillan.
LaBelle, M. (1980) *Alfred Jarry: Nihilism and the Theatre of the Absurd*,
    New York: New York University Press.
Lacan, J. (1968) *The Language of the Self*, New York: Dell.
—— (1982) *Feminine Sexuality*, London: Macmillan.
Laclau, E. and Mouffe, C. (1985) *Hegemony and Socialist Strategy*,
    London: Verso.
Lasch, C. (1980) *The Culture of Narcissism*, London: Sphere.
—— (1981) 'The Freudian left and the cultural revolution', *New Left
    Review* 129: 23–34.
Lash, S. and Urry, J. (1986) 'The dissolution of the social?' in M. Wardell
    and S. Turner (eds) *Sociological Theory in Transition*, London: Allen &
    Unwin.
—— (1987) *The End of Organised Capitalism*, Cambridge: Polity.
Lecourt, D. (1977) *Proletarian Science? The Case of Lysenko*, London:
    NLB.
Leenhardt, J. (1986) 'The role of the intellectual in France', *Postmodernism
    ICA Documents* 5: 63–5, London: ICA.

Lefebvre, H. (1971) *Everyday Life in the Modern World*, London: Allen Lane.

Levi, C. (1982) *Christ Stopped at Eboli*, Harmondsworth: Penguin.

Levin, C. (1984) 'Baudrillard, critical theory and psychoanalysis', *Canadian Journal of Political and Social Theory* 8 (1–2): 35–52.

Lévi-Strauss, C. (1969) *Conversations with Claude Lévi-Strauss*, London: Cape.

—— (1972) *The Savage Mind*, London: Weidenfeld & Nicolson.

Lipovetsky, G. (1975) 'Fragments energetiques apropos du capitalisme', *Critique* 379–94.

—— (1983) *L'Ere du Vide*, Paris: Gallimard.

Lukacs, G. (1978) 'On Walter Benjamin', *New Left Review* 110: 83–8.

Lukes, S. (1973) *Emile Durkheim*, Harmondsworth: Penguin.

Lunn, E. (1990) 'Beyond "mass culture" ', *Theory and Society* 19: 63–86.

Lyotard, J-F. (1984) *The Postmodern Condition: A Report on Knowledge*, Manchester: Manchester University Press.

Macchiocchi, A. (1973) *Letters From Inside the Italian Communist Party to Louis Althusser*, London: NLB.

Macherey, P. (1977) 'An Interview with P. Macherey', *Red Letters* 5: 3–9.

MacIntyre, A. (1970) *Marcuse*, London: Fontana.

Macksey, R. and Donato, E. (eds) (1972) *The Structuralist Controversy*, Baltimore: Johns Hopkins University Press.

McLuhan, M. (1967) *Understanding Media*, London: Sphere.

—— (1987) *Letters of Marshall McLuhan*, Oxford: Oxford University Press.

McRobbie, A. (1986) 'Postmodernism and popular culture', *Journal of Communication Inquiry* 10(2): 108–16.

Major-Poetzl, P. (1983) *Michel Foucault's Archaeology of Western Culture*, Brighton: Harvester.

Marcuse, H. (1955) *Eros and Civilization*, New York: Beacon.

—— (1968) *One Dimensional Man*, London: Sphere.

Marin, L. (1976) 'Disneyland: a degenerate utopia', *Glyph* 1(1): 50–66.

Marx, K. (1966) *Capital*, vol. 1, Moscow: Progress.

—— (1970) *Capital*, vol. 3, Moscow: Progress.

—— (1971) *A Contribution to the Critique of Political Economy*, London: Lawrence & Wishart.

—— (1973) *Grundrisse*, Harmondsworth: Penguin.

Mauss, M. (1966) *The Gift*, London: Cohen & West.

—— (1984) 'A sociological assessment of Bolshevism', *Economy and Society* 13(3): 331–74.

Mauss, M. (and Hubert, H. – this author's name is missing from the English edition) (1972) *A General Theory of Magic*, London: Routledge & Kegan Paul.

Merquior, J. (1986a) *From Prague to Paris*, London: Verso.

—— (1986b) 'Spider and bee: towards a critique of the postmodern ideology', *Postmodernism ICA Documents* 4: 16–18, London: ICA.

Midgely, M. (1984) *Wickedness*, London: Routledge.

Miller, D. (1987) *Material Culture and Mass Consumption*, Oxford: Blackwell.

Miller, J. (1971) *McLuhan*, London: Fontana.
—— (1981) *French Structuralism: A Multi-disciplinary Approach*, New York:,Garland.
Morris, M. (1988a) *The Pirate's Fiancée*, London: Verso.
—— (1988b) 'Banality in Cultural Studies', *Block* 14: 15–26.
Murray. D. (ed.) (1989) *Literary Theory and Poetry*, London: Batsford.
Nairn, T. (1988) *The Enchanted Glass*, London: Radius.
Niethammer, L. (1989) *Posthistoire: Ist die Geschichte zu End?*, Hamburg: Rowohlt.
Nietzsche, F. (1968) *Twilight of the Idols: The Anti-Christ*, Harmondsworth: Penguin.
—— (1969) *On the Genealogy of Morals. Ecce Homo*, New York: Vintage.
Nelson, C. and Grossberg, L. (eds) (1988) *Marxism and the Interpretation of Culture*, London: Macmillan.
Newman, M. (1986) 'Revising modernism, representing postmodernism: critical discourses of the visual arts', *Postmodernism ICA Documents* 4: 32–51, London: ICA.
Norris, C. (1989) 'Lost in the funhouse: Baudrillard and the politics of postmodernism', *Textual Practice* 3(3): 360–87.
O'Hara, Ɔ. (ed.) (1985) *Why Nietzsche Now?*, Bloomington: Indiana University Press.
Parsons, T. (1978) *Action Theory and the Human Condition*, Glencoe: Free Press.
Poirier, R. (1989) 'America deserta', *London Review of Books* 11(4): 3–4.
Popper, K. (1972) *Conjectures and Refutations*, 2nd edn., London: Routledge & Kegan Paul.
—— (1986) *Unended Quest*, London: Fontana.
Poster, M. (1975) *Existential Marxism in Postwar France: From Sartre to Althusser*, New Jersey: Princeton University Press.
—— (1981) 'Technology and culture in Habermas and Baudrillard', *Contemporary Literature* 22(4): 456–76.
Poulantzas, N. (1967) 'Marxist political theory in Great Britain', *New Left Review* 43: 57–74.
Pribram, E. (ed.) (1988) *Female Spectators*, London: Verso.
Punter, D. (ed.) (1986) *Introduction to Contemporary Cultural Studies*, London: Longman.
Racevskis, K. (1979) 'The theoretical violence of a catastrophical strategy', *Diacritics* 33–42.
—— (1980) 'The discourse of Michel Foucault', *Humanities and Society* 3(1): 41–53.
Rattansi, A. (1989) (ed.) *Ideology, Method and Marx*, London: Routledge.
Richman, M. (1982) *Reading Georges Bataille*, Baltimore: Johns Hopkins University Press.
Riviere, J. (1986) 'Womanliness as masquerade', in V. Burgin, J. Donald and C. Kaplan (eds) *Formations of Fantasy*, London: Methuen.
Rojek, C. (1990) 'Baudrillard and leisure', *Leisure Studies* 9: 7–20.
Rundell, J. (1987) *Origins of Modernity*, Cambridge: Polity.
Sahlins, M. (1974) *Stone Age Economics*, London: Tavistock.

Sanday, P.R. (1981) *Female Power and Male Dominance*, Cambridge: Cambridge University Press.

Sartre, J-P. (1957) *Being and Nothingness*, London: Methuen.

—— (1963) *The Problem of Method*, London: Methuen.

Schor, N. (1987) *Reading in Detail*, London: Methuen.

Serres, M. (1990) 'Entretien: M. Serres, la traversee des savoirs', *Magazine Littéraire*, 276: 98–103.

Soper, K. (1981) *On Human Needs*, Brighton: Harvester.

Sprinker, M. (1987) *Imaginary Relations*, London: Verso.

Starobinski, J. (1971) *Les Mots sous Les Mots, Les Anagrammes de Ferdinand de Saussure*, Paris: Gallimard.

Stauth, G. and Turner, B.S. (1988) *Nietzsche's Dance: Ressentiment, Reciprocity and Resistence in Social Life*, Oxford: Blackwell.

Stearn, G. (ed.) (1968) *McLuhan Hot and Cool*, Harmondsworth: Penguin.

Steiner, G. (1969) *Language and Silence*, Harmondsworth: Penguin.

Stewart, I. (1990) *Does God Play Dice*, Harmondsworth: Penguin.

Styron, W. (1970) *Set This House on Fire*, London: Cape.

Tafuri, H. (1989) *History of Italian Architecture, 1944–85*, London: MIT Press.

Thomas, K. (1984) *Man and the Natural World*, Harmondsworth: Penguin.

Thompson, J. (1984) *Studies in the Theory of Ideology*, Cambridge: Polity.

Tymms, R. (1949) *Doubles in Literary Psychology*, Cambridge: Bowes & Bowes.

Valente, J. (1985) 'Halls of mirrors: Baudrillard on Marx', *Diacritics* summer: 54–65.

Veblen, T. (1959) *The Theory of the Leisure Class*, New York: Mentor.

Weber, M. (1965) *The Protestant Ethic and the Spirit of Capitalism*, London: Unwin.

Wernick, A. (1984) 'Sign and commodity; aspects of the cultural dynamic of advanced capitalism', *Canadian Journal of Political and Social Theory* 8(1–2): 17–33.

Willis, P. (1990) *Common Culture*, Milton Keynes: Open University Press.

Wollen, P. (1989) 'The Situationist international', *New Left Review* 174: 67–95.

Wollheim, R. (1975) 'Psychoanalysis and feminism', *New Left Review* 93: 61–9 (see also discussion and reply, in *NLR* 97(1976): 106–12).

Zizek, S. (1989) *The Sublime Object of Ideology*, London: Verso.

Zukin, S. (1988) 'The postmodern debate over urban form', *Theory, Culture and Society* 5: 431–46.

Zurbrugg, N. (1988) 'Baudrillard's *Amerique*, and the "abyss of modernity"', *Art and Text* 29: 40–63.

Zylberberg, J. (1986) *Masses et Postmodernite*, Paris: Meridiens Klincksieck.

Index

Printed in the United Kingdom
by Lightning Source UK Ltd.
113716UKS00001B/68